JAGGED ROCKS OF WISDOM—THE MEMO

OTHER BOOKS

ALSO FOR THE LAW STUDENT

The Art of the Law School Transfer: A Guide to Transferring
Law Schools (forthcoming 2009)

Later-in-Life Lawyers: Tips for the Non-Traditional Law Student

Law School: Getting In, Getting Good, Getting the Gold

Planet Law School II: What You Need to Know (*Before* You Go)—
but Didn't Know to Ask...and No One Else Will Tell You

The Slacker's Guide to Law School: Success Without Stress

FOR THE SUMMER AND NEW ASSOCIATE

The Insider's Guide to Getting a Big Firm Job: What Every
Law Student Should Know About Interviewing

Jagged Rocks of Wisdom: Professional Advice for the
New Attorney

The Young Lawyer's Jungle Book: A Survival Guide

NON–LAW ADVENTURES

Grains of Golden Sand: Adventures in War-Torn Africa

Training Wheels for Student Leaders: A Junior Counseling
Program in Action

JAGGED ROCKS OF WISDOM—THE MEMO

MASTERING THE LEGAL MEMORANDUM

MORTEN LUND

THE FINE PRINT PRESS

HONOLULU

Copyright © 2009 by Morten Lund

Published by
The Fine Print Press, Ltd.
Honolulu, Hawaii
Website: www.fineprintpress.com
Email: info@fineprintpress.com

Library of Congress Cataloging-in-Publication Data

Jagged Rocks of Wisdom—The Memo: Mastering the Legal
    Memorandum / Morten Lund, Lawyer.
        p. cm.
    Includes index.
    ISBN 978-1-888960-08-2 (978-1-888960 : alk. paper)
    1. Legal composition. 2. Legal research—United States. I. Title.
II. Title: Mastering the Legal Memorandum.
KF250.L86 2009
808'.06634--dc22

                                        2008053984

Cover design and typesetting by Designwoerks, Wichita, Kansas.

The text face is Esprit Book, designed by Jovica Veljoviç and issued by ITC in 1985; supplemented with chapter headings in Castellar, designed by John Peters and issued by Monotype in 1957, section headings in Poppl-Laudatio, designed in 1982 by Friedrich Poppl for the H. Berthold AG Typefoundry of Berlin, and accent uses of American Typewriter, Helvetica Neue, and Law & Order.

PRINTED IN THE UNITED STATES OF AMERICA
19 18 17 16 15 14 13 12 11 10 09   10 9 8 7 6 5 4 3 2 1

CONTENTS

ACKNOWLEDGMENTS

I thank the various proofreaders and unofficial editors who helped me assemble this book. There were many, but Paul Bargren, Jeremy Polk, David Clark, Jim Clark, and Kesav Mohan were especially helpful. And, of course, I thank the numerous summer associates and junior associates who unwittingly contributed to the book. Mostly, however, my thanks for this book go to Thane Messinger, whose idea it was in the first place, and who inspired me to continue writing for junior associates.

FOREWORD

One of the key tasks for a new attorney is the legal memorandum. It would not be much of an overstatement to write that writing the perfect memorandum is the single most important skill (set of skills, really) for a new attorney.

Why? Because the memo is far more than a mere "research paper," such as one does countless times in college or graduate school, and it is vastly different from the occasional papers and law review note done in law school. First, the memo is a document with a singular purpose: to confirm a point of law. Second, this means more than it might seem, because the "point of law" is not an intellectual curiosity—it is a precise, definitive answer to a question posed by a client's situation. Third, this answer is important because that is the very essence of why the client is there. They don't want a "research paper," and they are hardly willing to pay for one. They do want an answer to a question— say, whether or not they can avoid the $2,500,000 penalty for terminating a joint venture, whether or not they will be granted a zoning variance that will make the difference between the two-hundred-fifty-million-dollar development being commercially viable or not (and thus whether they've just blown hundreds of thousands of dollars in fees, including lawyer's fees, and millions in interest payments, on preliminary work), or whether or not they will go to jail. *That* they are willing to pay for.

For the above reasons it is crucially important to understand why you are being asked to write that memo. You will conduct research, sweat over whether you're on the right track (or even near the right track), revise and re-revise countless times, and generally begin to question whether and when the Impostor Police will burst through the firm's library doors well past midnight as you sit there transfixed amidst the twelfth revision. All of these are true, and if you're doing your job right you darned well *ought* to feel all of the above, at least some of the time.

Part of the reason you should be nervous is that the partners for whom you toil are nervous. They either want to confirm that nagging question—possibly something raised over a casual conversation with a colleague, bringing the same hair-raising dread as when you heard something in your law school hallway that made you wonder whether you had been attending the right class—or they truly aren't sure of a legal point, adversary's counterpoint, or even legal strategy. They want, and need, a legal answer. It is you who will provide them that answer.

For all of these reasons, partners are insanely serious about memos. So too must you be. (Both serious and, to a large degree, insanely so.)

Looked at another way, think of how much weight might be placed on the result of the memo you are asked to write. In law school, questions popped up with happy abandon—in class, in hallways, in bed. (Okay, sometimes not-so-happy abandon.) In any location...the answer was right, the answer was wrong. Who cared? In law school, if you could frame the case—or at least sound convincing in framing the case—that was good enough.

In law practice, it no longer is. In fact, everything you were told in law school about learning how to think like a lawyer, focusing more on the reasoning and not the "answer" (which professors steadfastly shifted with each new twist in a hypo)...all of these are turned on their head when you are actually working in a firm. Why? Because the firm exists not to educate a class of neophytes, or tickle a professor's fancy, or play with one's mental self. The firm exists to serve a client.

The client will be served if their legal interest is served. Their legal interest will be served if they are told the law. They will be told the law if the answer is correct...both legally correct and correctly arranged within a range of correct contexts specific to that client. Despite the mind-numbing complexities and importance of deriving the right legal answer in a single memo, such a memo is just a part—often a small part—of the bigger picture. The correctness of the real answer—in the sense of whether the right question is being asked, right strategy employed, and so on—is almost out of your hands. Almost. It is in the minds of the firm's partners and senior associates, who are framing their legal analysis within a broader context of any number of other factors specific to that client and, often, a years-long relationship. You play no or almost no part of this. Yet you will be held to a correct answer in all senses and contexts.

Your task is at once both simpler and vastly more frightening. It is simpler because it is (usually but not always) a single question, with a single answer (even if that answer is "it depends..."). It is frightening because so much is riding on that answer—for both client (immediately) and for you (in perpetuity), and because it is within a context that is mostly hidden to you.

Morten Lund is the answer. Or, more cautiously, he is a way to get to the answer. His first book, *Jagged Rocks of Wisdom: Professional Advice for the New Attorney,* is a conversation (well, a drill instructor's stern lecture) that every new attorney should be forced to hear.

Why should being "forced" to hear a stern lecture be a good thing? Because it is. Law practice in a big firm especially is an extreme version of any high-stress, professional job. Almost no one goes into such a job truly prepared. One either survives after numerous office encounters, or one does not. Most do not.

Few new attorneys are fortunate enough to hear the message Morten has to say—*before* those encounters—and so reading it is the only reasonable substitute. Actually, it's far better, as partners really do not like being drill instructors. (Well, most of them.) They just want the !#*&%!!! answer.

This book is the answer—or a path to the answer—for the many memos you will be asked to write. In this, your long-term future at the firm is crucially dependent upon how well and quickly you develop expertise in an area (*i.e.,* how well you internalize and build upon the research done for those many memos), and in how well you interact with partners, clients, associates, secretaries, staff, vendors, vagrants, and various passers-by.

The second set of variables—mastering those interactions— is the subject of Morten's first book. The first part—actually writing that perfect memo—is why he wrote this one.

In the spirit of helping to put you in the right frame of mind (which will be some 49% of your success), here's an anecdote that might seem a bit odd, even comical. While it's about a famous political figure—this version, at any rate—this is in exactly the spirit of writing a legal memo. Thus it should be in your spirit.

> During the Nixon administration, U.S. Secretary of State Henry Kissinger was assigned a new intern.
>
> Eager to impress Dr. Kissinger (who before his public role had long been an academic star with a first-rate intellectual reputation), the intern wrote a report on a topic that Kissinger needed to research. Sometime later, when he asked Kissinger if he liked the report, the Secretary of State responded, "Is that the best you can do?"
>
> Startled at this response, the young intern replied that, yes, there were a few places he could improve on. He subsequently resubmitted the new, improved report to Kissinger. Again, when he encountered Kissinger in the hall he asked about the report. The intern got the same answer as before. Frustrated, he spent the next week double-checking every fact, proofreading every word, and making every improvement that he could think of, until…it…was…*perfect.*
>
> He re-resubmitted his now-masterpiece to the Secretary's office. The next day he saw Kissinger as he was leaving his office. Anxiously he asked his question. Kissinger flatly responded, "Is that the best you can do?"

At that point the intern all but lost it, barking at his new boss, "Yes, dammit. There isn't a person on your staff who could write a better or more complete report!"

To which Kissinger replied, "Good, then I'll read it."

This is the level you should reach for in your work in a law firm. There is no "almost." There is no "a few places where this could be improved." There's not even "best you can do." There is only one standard: that standard is *perfect*.

You're smart. Very smart. Yet your new bosses—the firm's law partners—are smart too. And they have a dozen years or more of actually doing what it is we only talk about in law school. And they have demanding and impatient clients to contend with, day in and day out, along with a firm to run. Understanding the difference your attention and attitude make will be crucial to your memo and to whether you will be asked to do the next one. That, of course, is important to whether you will be around at that firm to be asked.

I wrote in the foreword to Morten's first book that he had done a tremendous service to a new generation of attorneys, as indeed he had. Again, Morten has laid a nearly priceless gift before you: the gift of knowing how. Not just how to write that memo. Knowing how to write that memo such that *you* set the bar. In other words, knowing how to succeed.

In that journey, I wish you the very best.

Thane Messinger
Law School: Getting In, Getting Good, Getting the Gold
The Young Lawyer's Jungle Book: A Survival Guide
November 2008

INTRODUCTION

This is not a legal writing guide or a research guide. While I will touch on legalese and research methodology, I will not focus on proper punctuation, when to use the passive voice, the latest Bluebooking tips, or getting the most out of WestLaw. This is not a guide on "how to write a memo." Or, this is not *just* a guide on how to write a memo.

Instead, this is a guide to writing the *right* memo. This is a guide to understanding what the partner wants, even when he doesn't tell you. This is a guide to understanding the role of the legal memorandum within the confines of a law firm or legal department, and understanding the true nature of your job. This is a guide to help you succeed in the early stages of your legal career.

This guide presumes that you are already familiar with the English language, that you are capable of writing intelligent sentences, that your reading comprehension is decent, and that you have fundamental legal research skills. What this guide does *not* presume is any familiarity with or understanding of "the real world" of law or business, or experience with partners who place demands upon you that are at once unreasonable and unclear. This is a guide for intelligent, well-educated people who suddenly find themselves in unfamiliar waters where they are expected to teach themselves how to swim.

As with *Jagged Rocks of Wisdom: Professional Advice for the New Attorney*, I use the word "partner" loosely in this book: a "partner" is anyone with authority to boss you around. In other words, just about everybody, including associates just a year or two your senior. As a summer associate or junior associate, your job is to make the "partners" happy, including the "partners" who are not actual partners.

The examples and anecdotes in this book are real. The facts have been tweaked to be less recognizable, but each incident happened almost exactly as described. The summer associates described in the examples are actual summer associates making actual summer associate mistakes, which are pretty much the exact same mistakes made by junior associates. The mistakes I describe myself as having made are—sadly—mistakes that I actually made. I learned from my mistakes. I encourage you to learn from my mistakes as well.

The examples and anecdotes are often painfully obvious violations of the rule in question, and you might scoff at the fool who committed such a silly, yet grave, error. This is a mistake. The examples are illustrations, and are obvious on purpose. Most violations of the rules are not this obvious, and can be very subtle indeed. It is the subtle errors that are the enemy. You may never know that you committed such an error, and the partner might not even be able to put her finger on why the memo doesn't seem quite right. But the error was still committed, and you will have missed an opportunity to write a better memo.

As with *Jagged Rocks of Wisdom: Professional Advice for the New Attorney*, some of you will find many of my rules obvious. Good for you. Others will find that they have already broken most of the rules in this book, as many rules seem obvious only in retrospect.

A critic once wrote that my advice was obvious to anyone who understands the economics of the working world. I couldn't agree more—but the reality is that most fresh law graduates in fact do *not* understand the economics of the working world, even when they think they do. If these rules were as obvious as they appear, I would not have felt compelled to write this book, as I would not see and hear about these errors over and over and over again.

The rules in this book will occasionally be not just inconsistent and contradictory with each other, but also inconsistent and contradictory with the rules from *Jagged Rocks of Wisdom*.

That's how reality works. You can sit and complain about how the rules contradict each other, or you can go about the business of understanding how and why they contradict each other. Once you understand this, you are well on your way to understanding how to be a successful junior associate—and in time a successful senior associate and partner.

My hope is to present important information that is not special or secret, or even particularly complicated, but that somehow we fail to convey to our junior associates early on. Much like your job, these rules can be harsh and unreasonable and, as mentioned, seemingly impossible.

Your job is to navigate these jagged rocks of impossibility, and I hope in this book to provide you with helpful navigation in your efforts.

Good luck.

Lessons From
The First Book

Many reading this book will already have read *Jagged Rocks of Wisdom: Professional Advice for the New Attorney*. The lessons from that book apply to the writing of legal memoranda as much as to any other part of life in a law office. I of course encourage you to buy multiple copies of that book (and this one too), and then recommend both to your friends and enemies alike.

This book is essentially a companion to and continuation of the first book, and I have attempted to minimize repetition of the lessons from that book. Some of those lessons, however, are particularly important in the context of legal memoranda, and must therefore be repeated:

RULES 1 AND 2: PROOFREAD AND PROOFREAD AGAIN

Proofreading is important in everything you do, and the memos you will spend much of your time as a junior associate writing will provide ample opportunity for you to apply (or fail to apply) your proofreading skills. A memo may appear to be "only" an internal document of little importance, and therefore not worthy of your full attention to detail. This, of course, is false, but it is also irrelevant—if your work product consists largely of internal memoranda, then you will largely be judged based on the content and presentation of those internal memoranda, regardless of how "unimportant" they are. Few things can destroy partners' confidence in your abilities faster than memos full of typos.

RULE 5: JUST SAY NO TO PRELIMINARY REPORTS

Never will you face more pressure to provide preliminary reports than when you are researching and writing a memo. The more substantive the memo and the longer the research, the greater the pressure. Partners will be hounding you for results, and often it will seem that they care not if the results are accurate. This is pressure you must resist. If you provide a preliminary report that turns out to be incorrect (as they all too often end up being), no one will remember that they asked for an early answer. They will only remember that you were wrong.

RULE 7: THIS IS NOT SCHOOL; THIS IS NOT HOMEWORK

You have spent much of your educational career writing papers of various kinds. English papers, research papers, book reports, and so forth. In each case the purpose of the exercise was to demonstrate to the teacher/professor what you knew or had learned. In each case it was assumed that the instructor was already familiar with the subject matter of the paper, and you were not trying to educate him on the actual subject. In the law firm, the opposite is true. You get no kudos for trying hard or for showing off. Nobody cares how educational the process was for you. The partner, on the other hand, does not already know the answer. Or he does not know the precise answer, confirmed with rock-solid, up-to-that-day's-date research. He is counting on you to tell him. The purpose of the exercise is not to showcase your intellect, but to actually educate the reader.

RULE 12: ASK STUPID QUESTIONS, NOT LAZY QUESTIONS

A memo is almost always a research undertaking of some kind. Whether it is a legal research memo, a contract summary memo, or a patent evaluation memo, the basic purpose of the exercise is for you to obtain some information and then present that information. What a memo is *not*, therefore, is an opportunity for you to ask the partner the questions that you are supposed to be researching. If you are asked to evaluate the default/termination provisions of a contract, you should not ask the partner which sections contain those provisions—that is exactly what she just asked you to do. Yes, the partner could have done the research herself, but she asked you, and you do not get to delegate back to the partner. If you are stuck and need guidance that is one thing; not bothering to look first—and look carefully—is something else entirely.

THE RULES

Rule Number 1

Proofread

Proofreading is important.

Yes, I know I mentioned this in the introduction. Yes, I know I mentioned it (twice) in the first book. And I am mentioning it again now. I will probably mention it again in every book. You should take the hint. Proofreading is important—*very* important. None of the other advice in this book is meaningful unless you proofread your work to make sure you actually apply the rules.

Proofreading takes two forms, both of which must be undertaken with equal care and diligence: The first is "low" proofreading, which is essentially copy-editing. This does not sound glamorous, but that does not make it any less important. A misspelled word, no matter how harmless, directly and correctly conveys to the reader that you did not try hard enough.

The second form of proofreading is "high" proofreading, which is your last chance at quality control. High proofreading gives you an opportunity to make sure that you do not have sentence remnants, thought remnants, or research remnants. It gives you an opportunity to check the flow of the document and the flow of the logic.

Proofreading is an opportunity to see the forest as well as the trees. Proofreading is not merely an opportunity to avoid errors, but an opportunity to affirmatively improve the quality of your work. The sentence that seemed brilliant when you wrote it may no longer make sense in the context of the finished memo. You will not know this unless you proofread, and then proofread again.

Proofreading gives you an opportunity to just make sure. Proofreading gives you peace of mind—because writing a good document only takes you halfway there. Proofreading not only gives you a good document, but makes you confident that you have a good document. A properly proofread memorandum is a memorandum you can feel confident about. Few things will throw you off kilter quicker when discussing your memo than being confronted with an obvious mistake. Not only has the partner's confidence in you been eroded, but *your* confidence in you has been eroded.

So proofread.

A properly proofread document shows the reader that you are diligent and that you care. It shows the reader that you took the time to do the job right. Documents with typos do not inspire confidence, and confidence does not distinguish between typos and research quality. The partner either will or will not have confidence in your work as a whole, and typos can diminish that confidence just as quickly as flawed conclusions, if not faster. The partner will usually not know the precise answer to the question presented in your memo, and might therefore not immediately spot the flawed conclusion, but he will almost certainly know good spelling from bad. If I see a memo riddled with typos or poor sentence structure, I can and will conclude that the writing was sloppily done, and that I can and will extrapolate freely that the research was equally sloppily done, and that I can therefore not trust the conclusions. As a result I will think less of you for it.

So proofread.

Failure to proofread properly is perhaps the single most common error among summer associates and junior associates, yet it is also the easiest to fix. Unlike many of the other errors committed by junior associates, you already have the tools to stop the typos, but many fail to do so. I emphasize proofreading above all else because it is something we all have the power to do, if we take it seriously enough. Yes, I want you to finish the memo on an unreasonably short timeline. Yes, I know you worked hard to understand the underlying issue. I don't care. If I encounter a typo in the first paragraph, I lose all confidence that you did the job properly. Proofreading helps me, but most of all it helps you.

As a junior associate I was working on a rush research project regarding the authority of managers of limited liability companies. My research was thorough, my writing solid, and the conclusion likely to make the client happy.

The partner gave me a few minor comments and asked me to send the final memo directly to the client as soon as possible. I made the revisions, ran some quick word-searches to check for consistency, and sent the memo off to the client, happy with a good day's work.

Less than half an hour later, the client called the partner to ask why they had a memo discussing "mangers."

In my haste to get the memo out the door, I had managed to hit "replace all" while searching through the document, changing "manager" to "manger" throughout.

The client did not see the humor in the situation, and did not care about the brilliance of my analysis.

Rule Number 2

Answer The Question

So you wrote a great memo. You researched carefully, you wrote carefully, you proofread carefully. You are proud and confident in your work. You look forward to discussing the memo with the partner.

You cheerfully knock on the partner's door, and you are met with an annoyed scowl as she asks you to close the door behind you.

How could this be? You are absolutely certain that your memo (for once) is flawless. Quite simply, as the partner is about to explain, you answered the wrong question. It was indeed a great memorandum, but a great memorandum on the wrong issue. She needed to know the answer to Question "X," and after reading your memo she still needs to know the answer to Question "X."

How do you ensure that you are actually answering the correct question? Simple: You make sure that you understand the question to begin with. Repeat the question back to confirm. Ask background questions to make sure that you understand the question the same way the partner does.

Yes, you might feel a little silly repeating back what you were just told. Yes, the partner may appear impatient or dismissive. But yes, it is still a good idea. The partner has not been a junior associate for a very long time, and has long since forgotten just how deep your ignorance runs. When she asks a question, she will subconsciously assume that you understand the thrust of the question, the purpose of the question, and simply the meaning of the question. She will assume that you understand her acronyms, vague statutory references, and passing mentions of fundamental principles of law. Moreover, you yourself are also woefully ignorant of just how woeful your ignorance is. You may think you understand the question when you

do not. You and the partner come from entirely different starting points, and it is incumbent upon *you* to make sure that you
truly understand your assignment.

Of equal importance: write the question down. The exact
question, verbatim. On your legal pad, in black-and-white. And
write down the additional references the partner is likely to toss
out in response to your questions. Every one. Try to write
quickly, but do not skip anything for fear of being thought slow.
Be deliberate. A few extra seconds here can save you, in more
ways than one.

I continue to be amazed at the number of summer associates
and junior associates who think they can remember everything.
Often their memory is quite impressive—they may get it 95%
right. But in the practice of law we have a word for 95% right.
That word is "wrong."

> As part of a due diligence effort, a summer associate was
> asked to summarize the assignment provisions in a box full
> of contracts, to determine whether our pending acquisition
> would trigger consent requirements.
>
> The resultant memorandum did a fine job of summariz-
> ing the assignment provisions, but only as to whether the
> other party needed consent to assign, not our side.
>
> The entire review had to be redone.

Answering a question that is almost the question asked is
just as useless as answering a completely unrelated question. I
asked that specific question because that was the specific question at hand, not because I was looking for information on the
general subject matter. I will not be impressed with your mastery of the subject if you did not answer my question.

A memo that fails to answer the question I asked is worse
than useless. It is a waste of time and resources. It will throw off
schedules and cause embarrassment. It cannot be billed to the
client. Yes, it is my responsibility to make sure that you under-

stand your assignment—but it is also *your* responsibility to make sure that you understand your assignment.

My failure to communicate does not excuse your failure to comprehend.

Rule Number 3

Answer The *Real* Question

I just finished telling you to always answer the question asked. Now I am going to tell you to not always answer the question asked.

More specifically, you have to understand what the question asked is trying to achieve. The problem we face when formulating research assignments is that—by definition—we do not know what we are looking for. As a result, it is often difficult to state the question correctly, or even to state the correct question at all. Other times I may just do a sloppy job of stating my question, or I may forget that you are not familiar with the case or transaction, and assume that you know what I am talking about.

A client believed he was being illegally persecuted by government officials.

A summer associate was asked to research the various process options for pursuing remedies against the officials in question, should we decide the case merited action.

The resulting memo exactly answered my stated question: it briefly described each possible process option. It was completely free of typos, was nicely organized, and generally well written.

It was also useless.

The memo failed to address my real (and unstated) question of which of these options would be best suited for our case and why, and which options would be more difficult to pursue.

The memo provided a brief listing of easily available information, but the information completely failed to tell me what I needed to know.

Either way, you cannot assume that the question I asked is the question I should have asked. You must read between the lines. You must be able to see the real purpose, the real goal, and move the ball toward that goal. You are the one doing the research. That makes YOU the expert, not me. I am looking for you to educate me on the subject, not the other way around. If I knew the answer I would not have asked you to go look it up. You are doing the research, you are gaining the knowledge. If in the course of your research you come to learn that I may not have asked the right question—take note! This is important. Your job is not merely to answer my uneducated or sloppy question, but to help me with my actual question, whether or not I bothered to tell you to do so.

Part of your job as an attorney is not just to do what the client says, but to tell them when they are wanting the wrong thing, or are forgetting to want something. If we just blindly did the client's bidding we would not be advisors, but research assistants. When asked a question, lawyers love to answer the question with "Wrong question. You should be asking X." This starts for you right now. The partners in the firm are your clients, and your job is to help them with their actual needs, not merely slavishly follow their exact directions.

If you simply follow my instructions, you will fail.

Importantly, this does *not* mean that you can casually decide to abandon the question asked, and reshape the assignment to your liking. Nor can you casually and bluntly tell the partner that he is asking the wrong question. You do not have the authority to unilaterally change the scope of your assignment. To the contrary, you are still bound by the partner's express instructions. Yet you cannot assume that those express instructions are the extent of your assignment.

Rule #2 still applies—you must Answer The Question. But phrase your answer in a manner to also address the unasked question(s). Move the ball forward. Do not simply provide dead information. Place it in context. I can read too—if I wanted you to just recite the statute, I would have looked it up myself. As you are answering the question asked, keep in mind the possibility that the question asked and the real question might not be the same. Answer both.

Should it turn out that the stated question is thoroughly wrong, bring it to the partner's attention. Do not unilaterally change the assignment. Discuss your initial findings with the partner, and determine what the correct new question should be. If you write a great memo answering the real question but ignoring the stated question, the partner will not be happy. Rule #2 applies. If, on the other hand, you write that same great memo answering the real question, but only after discussing the change in direction with the partner, the partner will be twice impressed: not only did you write a great memo, but you identified the incorrect path you were on and brought it to her attention.

A midlevel associate asked a summer associate to draft a memo discussing potential contract claims and the related procedural issues in the event of a dispute.

The memo did all of that, but failed to mention (or discuss) the contract's arbitration provision.

Usually, however, the question will not be thoroughly wrong. Instead, the question will quite often be mostly right— just not exactly right. Now your task is more difficult. Partners generally do not want to have philosophical discussions about delicate nuances of the questions posed. Partners just want you to answer the darn question. On the other hand, it is incumbent upon you to make sure that you are not off on a wild goose chase. So…you must apply Rule #2 *and* Rule #3. Answer the question, but also provide information that is relevant to what you believe is the real question. If you cannot do both in a straightforward manner, then the real question is far enough afield that you need to obtain clarification. You need to make the determination of whether you need further guidance, and you need to do so in such a manner that (a) you will always be right, and (b) you do not come across as helpless or clueless.

Should the partners do a better job of stating the questions? Yes. Should the partners educate themselves a little before even asking the questions, so as to ask intelligent questions? Perhaps. Does it matter what the partners should have done? No. You are the one writing the memo, and you are the one who will be judged on its content, quality, and usefulness. It is *your* responsibility to make the memo as useful as it can possibly be. Washing your hands of the memo with "I did what I was told" is simply insufficient.

Rule Number 4

Understand The Context: One Size Does Not Fit All

"Memo" is a rather generic term. It is used loosely by attorneys in different practice areas to describe very different things. Outside of the practice of law, a "memo" can mean a whole host of things, often relating to internal communications. There is the memo from management regarding the strategic plan, the memo from HR regarding changes to the 401(k) plan, the memo from the mail room regarding new pickup times. These types of memos exist in virtually every organization, including law firms. These memos are *not* what this book is about.

The "memo" I am describing in this book is the *legal* memo. This type of memo is generally a research effort of some kind. But even with the "legal research memo" category there is significant variety. The thing being researched, the purpose of the research, and the presentation of the research—each will be different from all the others, depending on your context. You must adjust.

Within the firm, every department, every practice area, has its own mentality, its own purpose, its own way of operating. In law school it sometimes seems as if all lawyers do is research complex case law dilemmas on weighty issues and write up lengthy analytical discussions. Reality, however, is quite different.

If you happen to be in the litigation department, you will probably be doing a fair amount of caselaw research. But it will not be constitutional law. Instead, you may be dragged into the middle of an ongoing case that started while you were in college. After years of discovery and preliminary motions, a trial is on the horizon—but not today. Today, we have to determine whether the prongs of intentional interference are different in Nevada than in New York, because we are filing briefs next Wednesday. You must understand this in order to understand *why* you are doing your memo—and what the partner is trying to achieve.

If you are not in the litigation department, things will be even more different from law school. In a business law department (these go by many different names in different firms), you may be asked to do research that smells a lot like litigation research, but isn't. In the business law department we do not want to win a case—we want there never to be a case at all. Every department, every practice...each has its own purpose, its own goal. It is absolutely imperative that you understand this purpose and this goal, and that you operate as a member of *your* department, and not operate as if you are just on loan from another group.

As a summer associate, I spent the first half of the summer assigned to the litigation department, and the second half assigned to the business law department.

Early in my stint in the business law department, a partner was describing the challenging relationship our manufacturer client was having with a dealer, and I was to research dealership law to determine whether we could terminate the dealer.

I was still in litigation mode from my time in the litigation department. During the entire discussion I was distracted as I waited for the partner to say "... and then we filed the lawsuit." This never happened.

I took the same mentality to the research memo, and produced a detailed discussion of numerous complicated theories that would provide weak-but-defensible arguments that would cleverly allow us to drag out the litigation when we got sued for wrongful termination.

The partner was neither impressed nor interested—he wanted to know if and how we could terminate without leading to litigation. I had answered his question, but in the wrong context.

Just as likely as caselaw research, you may be asked to summarize contracts or evaluate their provisions. This might be due diligence for an acquisition, or an evaluation of exit strategies for an unfavorable contract, or a comparative analysis for negotiation purposes. Or something else entirely, but something that has no caselaw in sight (or any other law, for that matter). This type of memo is still a research memo—just not a memo researching laws. Now you are researching contract provisions. In an intellectual property context, you may be asked to research laws and regulations to establish the validity of a patent, or the possibility of challenging the patent. While the context is different, the fundamental task is the same: Understand the problem, research the issue, and describe your conclusion.

Once you have established the context of your memorandum, you must address the issue in light of that context. Litigators have entirely different issues in mind than business lawyers, even when they ask you to research the exact same thing. It is not enough to understand the question I asked and the real question I meant to ask—you must also understand why I asked the question, and what I intend to do with the answer.

A litigation memo is very different from a business law memo, which is very different from a regulatory compliance memo or a tax strategy memo. You need to write the type of memo that is needed for that specific context. Writing a compliance memo in a litigation context is not helpful, nor is writing a litigation memo in a tax context.

This rule is essentially an application of Rule #3—Answer The *Real* Question. You will not be able to answer the real question unless you can identify the real question, and you will not be able to identify the real question unless you understand the context.

If we are in the middle of a lawsuit, your memo needs to be in the context of that lawsuit. Your research needs to be geared towards winning *that* lawsuit, not some theoretical other lawsuit. You need to identify cases that hurt or help your case and arguments and counter-arguments that might come into play. You need to jump into the stream of *that case*. Not just where the case is, but where it has been, how fast it is moving, where it is going, and why. Stating the law neutrally or in a vacuum is not helpful.

If we are operating within a contract but concerned about a potential lawsuit, you need to address the legal issues in the context of avoiding a lawsuit, or the likelihood of success in a lawsuit. This memo will not be incorporated into a brief, but will form the basis for evaluating the litigation risk. In the end, we must advise our client on a course of action, and your memo must contribute towards that advice. Clever long-shot arguments that may come into play in a lawsuit are not relevant to that discussion. And the discussion must be relevant to *that* contract, not merely to contracts in general.

I do not care about general investigations into issues. I want to know the answer to my question as it applies to MY case or MY deal. If you do not address the question in the specific context of my case or my deal, you are not addressing my question at all. Instead, you are accomplishing an expensive distraction and delay.

I asked a summer associate to review an exceedingly messy joint venture arrangement, and present and evaluate potential exit strategies for our client.

The summer associate's memo discussed and evaluated arguments that could be made before a court, and evaluated exit strategies in terms of supporting or not supporting these arguments.

Our client was not interested in litigation, and the best strategy was the one that would avoid litigation, not win litigation.

The memo did not address the likelihood that any given exit strategy would land us in court, which was the client's true concern.

The partner may simply ask you to "research" a particular issue. As you do so, you discover that the central principles of the issue are clearly established by a statute, or perhaps a few central cases, but that there are a myriad of finer points with their own set of cases. You have the option of asking the partner which, if any, of these finer points to chase down, but if you truly understand the context you won't have to, because you will already know.

Understanding the context and purpose of the memo (indeed, of any task) is a powerful tool that will turn you from a mindless research drone into an information-crunching machine and answer-synthesizer. Your memo needs not only to answer the stated question and the unstated question, but it needs to do so in the correct context and with the correct goal in mind.

If you write a business memo in a litigation context (or vice versa), I will think that you are not paying attention—and I will be right. If you write a litigation memo without addressing the actual lawsuit, I will think that you are wasting my time—and I will be right.

I do not read or mark up memos that are out of context. I stop reading after the first page, if not the first paragraph, and tell the associate to start over. My time has already been wasted, and I will not waste any more by reading the rest of your irrelevant memo. My files are full of draft memos that I never finished reading because the first page told me everything I needed to know: they were a useless waste of time and money, and had to be redone.

Your brilliant memo, with its excellent proofreading and thoughtful analysis, is a complete waste, for you and for me, if it is out of context.

Rule Number 5

Understand The Facts...
Even The Ones You Don't Know

The legal memorandum is not a discussion exercise. This is not a theoretical exploration or a law school hypo. We are not interested in "what if." I want the answer to MY question (both asked and unasked), not the answer to some other question. And in order for you to answer my question, you have to understand my facts.

A memo based on incorrect facts is useless.

A legal memorandum consists generally of a three-part process: understanding the facts, researching the law, and applying the law to the facts to reach a conclusion. Careful analysis of the preceding sentence will reveal why understanding the facts is important. But understanding the facts goes beyond even that. If you do not understand the facts, not only will you be unable to apply the law to such facts, but you will be unable to research the law in the first place, because the law itself is fact-specific. When you research whether a particular contract is enforceable, you will not even know whether to research offer/acceptance or public policy concerns unless you understand the facts. The law does not exist in a vacuum.

And, of course, if you write a memo based on incorrect facts, not only will you will have wasted your time and mine, but you will have demonstrated to me that (a) you were not paying attention when I was explaining things to you, and (b) you did not care about or understand what you were doing enough to realize that you did not have sufficient or correct facts.

Is it painfully obvious that you should understand the facts before researching and writing a legal memorandum? Yes it is...but that does not stop summer and junior associates from writing memos with only a cursory examination of the facts, and doing so on a regular basis. Do not let that be you.

How can this be? How can (presumably smart) attorneys and almost-attorneys fail to do something as basic as comprehend the facts? Simple: It's not that simple. This is not a law school exam. You are not handed two paragraphs labeled "The Facts" which encompass the entire universe of known facts, beyond which you are entitled to assume without limitation or repercussion.

The real world is fuzzy, and so are the facts. Maybe you were given a banker's box full of documents, with the instructions that "everything you need to know should be in there." Or, more likely, you were told that there is a box somewhere in the fileroom with everything you need to know. Of course, there will be plenty of irrelevant information in that box as well, and notice the "should"—the partner is not guaranteeing complete information. The partner probably does not *have* complete information. The partner will present basic background—it is up to *you* not only to comprehend the relevant facts, but to actually establish what the relevant facts are.

I asked a senior associate (who should have known better) to advise me on a technical regulatory matter, to determine whether a particular transaction structure would pass regulatory muster.

Significant research was involved, and a lengthy memorandum was prepared over the course of a couple of weeks.

Coming from an experienced attorney, the memo was of course perfectly proofread, contained flawless logic stated very clearly, and was generally an excellent piece of work.

It also described the regulatory implications of a transaction structure different from my transaction in a small, but fundamental, manner. The memo, and much of the research, had to be completely redone.

Significant amounts of delay, expense, and embarrassment resulted.

Sometimes the real world is just complex. Your assignment may be to evaluate the indemnification provisions of a stock purchase agreement. The contract itself is 78 pages long, with four inches worth of schedules and exhibits. You, of course, have never seen a stock purchase agreement before, or any contract this size for that matter. Conveniently, however, the partner pointed out that the indemnification provisions are in Section 15. That was nice of her, and makes your job much easier.

Except that she didn't mention that the survivability section addresses indemnification. Or that the limitation of liability addresses and limits indemnification. Or that several of the schedules expressly limit the applicability of indemnification under certain circumstances. And so forth. She didn't give you all the facts. Part of your task is to ascertain all the facts, to figure out which parts of the contract were relevant. If you write a memo based solely on Section 15, you will have written a memo based on incorrect facts. More bluntly, your memo will be *wrong,* and the partner, based on your memo, will give advice to the client that will also be wrong. "You didn't tell me to check the survivability section" is not a valid excuse. Your job as an attorney is to arrive at the correct result, not merely to analyze the facts you have been given.

Sometimes the partner will be able to spot the missing fact or incorrect assumption. If you explicitly state a fact in your memo that she recognizes as wrong, it can be corrected. If you base a conclusion on an unstated fact, quite likely no one will be the wiser until it is too late. Don't roll the dice. Get the facts.

How do you get the facts? You get the facts by treating the facts as part of the research project, not as an immutable set of assumptions for your research project. The "facts" are not a fixed set that provides the backdrop for your legal research. Your task is to research the law *and* to research the facts. You are a sleuth, and your task is to reach a conclusion based on facts and law. You do not get to assume either the facts or the law at will, but instead you must research both.

Researching the facts may mean reading reams of documents, or backtracking correspondence, or going back to the partner or client with additional questions. When you do so, don't waste the partner's time: ask intelligent questions based on your research so far, and do not go on factual fishing expeditions in the partner's office.

The facts may change, or your need for particular facts may change, and you have to change with them. Most likely, you will not know which facts you need until you have begun researching the law, at which point you go back to find more facts, to which you then apply the law, and so forth.

Being a research sleuth does not make you a private detective, however. You have to stay within your mandate. Sometimes particular facts are required but not easily available, and this does not mean that you should spend endless hours (and client dollars) researching every single factoid. As with all research efforts, you must communicate with the partner if it appears that your fact research is becoming larger or more elaborate than anticipated.

Sometimes the correct answer is to assume facts and offer conditional conclusions. This is perfectly acceptable and appropriate, so long as your assumptions and conditions are logical and carefully identified, and are there for the convenience of the client rather than due to your own laziness.

Facts and law work together. They are not separate creatures that can be studied or researched without each other. In a law school exam you can often make up or hypothesize facts as you please, because a law school exam is a theoretical exercise. A real life legal memorandum is neither theoretical nor an exercise. Do not treat it as such.

Rule Number 6

Understand The Deadline:
The *Real* Deadline

Many recruiting staff will remind their summer associates to make sure to get a deadline for their projects. As a result, many summer associates (and junior associates) automatically end the project assignment conversation with "when do you need this by?"

This is not a bad thing. Having a deadline is a good thing. It keeps you motivated, lays expectations on the table, and generally levels the informational playing field.

Deadlines are also a trap. They lull you into a sense of false security, into believing that so long as you get the memo done by "the deadline," all will be well. This is usually true—but only sort of.

Half of the time, when summer associates ask me "when do you need this by," I take a guess at how long I think the project ought to take, and maybe add a day for good measure, and declare that the deadline. This deadline is "real" because I just declared it so, and you should therefore take it seriously…but it bears no real relationship to my actual timing requirement. Perhaps I really needed the information the week after next, or at some undetermined later time. But, no fool myself, I know what will happen to my project if I give a deadline of "later some time." So I make up an arbitrary deadline designed solely to make sure that you don't procrastinate too much.

Contrast this to the memo commissioned by a litigator who expects to incorporate your memo into her brief. The brief has a specific and absolute deadline, with dire consequences if the deadline is missed. This memo absolutely *must* be finished in time to be worked into the brief, or it is useless.

If you go blindly by what you were told, you will think these two deadlines are the same. In one sense they are—in the sense that your job as a junior associate is to meet all deadlines given to you—but in another sense they are entirely different, and if you have been paying attention and applying prior rules, thereby understanding the real question, the context, and the facts, you will also understand what these deadlines mean.

Before I go any further, let me be perfectly clear: This rule is *not* a license for you to prioritize work and selectively ignore deadlines. You are not authorized to prioritize work, and you are certainly not authorized to ignore deadlines. Yes, there may come a time when you can casually ask the partner with the made-up deadline for an extension. That time is not now. You have not yet earned the right to ask for extensions. And there will be a very long time until you can (casually or otherwise) decide which project should get top priority.

That is not what this rule is about.

This rule, like most of the rules in this book, is about helping you better meet the partner's needs by understanding what those needs are.

To go back to the previous example: If I arbitrarily declared that "sometime on Friday" is the deadline for the memo, then most likely I will be satisfied with 5:00 p.m. on Friday, just as much as if the memo were delivered at noon. Heck, Friday at 10:00 p.m. (or midnight) is probably fine too. I wasn't going to read it until Monday or Tuesday anyway.

If, on the other hand, the litigator told you that the memo was needed Friday morning, that might mean something else entirely. Her brief might be due Friday afternoon, and every hour—and sometimes every minute—counts. A memo delivered at 8:15 a.m. is significantly more helpful than a memo delivered at 11:15 a.m. Both memos technically meet the stated deadline, but one will make the partner *much* happier. A memo delivered at 11:59 a.m. might be too late to make it into the brief at all.

Or perhaps the brief is due on the following Monday instead of Friday. Even so, there is a significant difference between a memo delivered Friday at 8:00 a.m., or 12:00 noon, or 5:00 p.m. Every hour of delay on that memo is now one more hour the partner has to work over the weekend dealing with your memo. Making partners work extra on weekends is not a recipe for your success.

Now, if you had been listening, *really* listening, when the partner explained the project, perhaps even asking intelligent questions, you would have known what the deadline really meant. You would know which deadline was flexible and which was not, and which deadline it was important to not only meet, but actually beat. By paying attention and understanding what was really going on, you would be able not merely to do the minimum required, but to contribute to your real ability—and to the partner's goal of actually using your memo.

Delivering my "sometime on Friday" memo on Thursday night will not even register on my radar. Getting the litigator her "Friday morning" memo on Thursday afternoon will earn you a big gold star.

You are not alone in dealing with deadlines—deadlines are a part of daily life for attorneys. It is a sadly common practice in the practice of law to deliver memos (and other legal products) to clients "by the end of business"—*i.e.,* five-ish. This practice does the client few favors, since the client now has to look at the memo after hours, or wait until the next day. If the client actually needed the memo on that day (as opposed to a "whenever" memo), then 5:00 p.m. is not helpful. Now is the time for you to *not* develop this bad habit. Deliver the memos on a timeline to be helpful, not on a timeline to merely technically meet the stated deadline.

To complicate matters further, deadlines have a habit of changing. Usually they change by being extended or delayed, but not always. Perhaps the transaction was accelerated. Perhaps the partner decided to use your argument in THIS motion instead of saving it for later. Perhaps the client was able to get an earlier meeting with the government official. Either way, your deadline just went from "Friday" to "tomorrow" or even "right now."

> I brought a summer associate in on a rush project mid-day on a Friday.
>
> I needed some inserts for a memo drafted, and I needed to send my memo to the client Monday afternoon.
>
> I told the summer associate to have something to me by noon on Monday, which would be tight, but would give me enough time to make edits before forwarding my memo.
>
> Unprompted, the summer associate worked the weekend and sent me the inserts on Sunday, thereby making my Monday significantly less stressful, and allowing me to comfortably beat my client deadline.
>
> His understanding of the real deadline and the reasoning behind the stated deadline allowed him to be far more helpful than I had expected.

Again, understanding the nature of the deadline will better allow you to predict those shifts, which in turn will allow you to deal with them. Did you know which motions your memo might apply to? Did you know that there was an option to accelerate the government proceedings? Did you know that the client was considering changing his plans?

Often, you will have no idea. You are the junior associate, and people do not tell junior associates—and certainly not summer associates—about the inner politics of the deal. But even if no one tells you anything, if you know the purpose and intent of your memorandum, you will be able to evaluate the risk of sudden acceleration.

Sometimes the real deadline for a memorandum is "before the client calls to ask about it." The partner may give you a semi-arbitrary deadline, but that is the "I will be angry if I do not have the memo by then" deadline. The real deadline for you for this type of memo is "as soon as possible." When the client calls about the subject, the partner either will or will not have your memo in hand. It is a strictly binary scenario, and it will not matter whether you meet or miss the "official" deadline by a minute or a day. If the partner has the memo in hand when the client calls, he is happy. If the partner does not, he is not. This is your chance to make the partner look good. Part of your job is to make the partner look good. Take these opportunities when you can.

Understanding the true nature of the deadline given is as central as understanding the overall context—in fact, they are often one and the same. Deadlines are rarely simple "due by" delivery dates. Deadlines are part of the transactional canvas. Each memorandum has a role to fill, and timing is an important part of that role. Understanding the true nature of the deadline will allow you to operate as a full member of the team, rather than being simply an associate with a task.

RULE NUMBER 7

GET ON WITH IT ALREADY

Procrastination is always bad, and always tempting. As a successful student, you have no doubt mastered the skill of cramming several days' worth of work into the hours between midnight and 7:00 a.m. That was a bad idea in school, even when the results were acceptable. It is an even worse idea on the job, because the results will never be acceptable.

The reason is simple: In school, it was all about you. You were the one to develop the product, you did the research, you obtained (or invented) the facts, and you decided when the product was complete.

None of those apply any more.

As much as you would like to view "the memo" as a solitary effort, as a noble quest that you go off and finalize all by yourself, this is simply not true. Every legal matter will involve numerous people. There will be some times when some tasks can—and should—be done by yourself in a quiet room, but by and large you will be operating as part of a team. This specifically includes research memoranda. As much as the memo is your job, it is an interactive process, and you should expect to discuss issues of fact and law with other team participants on a regular basis. As a result, you need to consider not only your own schedule when working on a memo, but everybody else's.

You do not necessarily have to finish the memo ahead of schedule, but you absolutely must *start* the memo ahead of schedule.

In fact, I recommend starting the research immediately. *Now*. Even if you were in the middle of another project when you got the call, if at all possible spend at least a little time with the new project before continuing with the old one.

The facts and issues are fresh. This is your chance to move the information into long-term memory before it goes stale.

Review the notes, flip through the documents, crack a book or two—but start thinking about it *now*, while you have the benefit of a head full of useful knowledge.

Beyond that first refresher, your goal should be to keep the project moving. Do not let the memo become a "later" project. "Later" projects are always more difficult to pick back up, and some suffer more than others from the hiatus in attention. Memoranda suffer more than most. If you let the project slip your mind, you will have to re-teach yourself all the facts and issues, while trying to recall the subtle nuances of what exactly the partner wanted—including all of the crucially important background information such as the real deadline, real question, and so on.

But far more important than starting right away, more important than not letting the project slide, is not to delay beginning the project until you get close to that deadline. This is an interactive process, and you must interact. For most significant memos you will have some follow-up questions or clarifications that will only become clear after you have spent some time with the research. The project could balloon up or go completely sideways. You just do not know, and you will not know until you get your hands dirty.

I asked a summer associate a relatively simple question about withdrawal from a joint venture, and gave him a folder of documents to review.

The next day he informed me that the documents he needed were not in the folder. It turned out that those documents had been stored offsite, and it would take another day or two to get them.

By looking at the folder right away he was able to discover that documents were missing in time for us to find them and still answer the client's question on time.

Had he waited even a single day it would have been too late.

Time after time, junior associates swamped with too much work let a research project sit on their desk until the afternoon before the deadline. They then start working on it, and discover—*surprise!*—that they have questions for the partner. At this point, one of two things will happen. The associate slinks into the partner's office to ask a basic question, thereby broadcasting that she had not started the project until an hour ago. That is the better scenario. Quite often, however, what happens instead is that the associate discovers that the partner has gone home for the day, which forces the associate to choose between calling the partner at home (now with a doubly annoyed partner answering the phone), or missing the deadline to ask questions the next day, or delivering a memo without getting needed information.

None of those are good outcomes for you.

All of those will make you look bad, and will make it look like MY project is low on your list (which it was), and will make me doubt the quality of your work, since you obviously do not care enough to get going. I will also wonder whether you are interested in further work from me, since I am clearly the least important thing on your desk. You are not only endangering my confidence in your interest in this project, but your interest in doing work for me in the future. For your future at the firm, this is very, very bad—regardless of who I am, how forgiving I am, how much leeway we have with the client, how much damage this causes, or how interested I am in making (or breaking) your career.

And even this scenario assumes that everything goes according to plan—which it probably will not. You will quickly discover that sometimes a four-hour project becomes a four-day project. Had you started the project right away you would have known that with four days yet to go. Plenty of time to adjust your work schedule, or even discuss your schedule and the project with me. Asking for a time extension is not easy, but asking for an extension the night before your memo is due does not qualify as merely "not easy."

Fine—so you start one day earlier. Still not good enough. Yes, you are less likely to spend the night coming up with sub-par product, but I still remember assigning the project to you a week ago, and five days have gone by without any questions. Now, suddenly, you are asking basic questions that make it quite obvious that you just started work on the project. While I am not at the very bottom of your list, my relative importance (or lack thereof) is still crystal clear to me.

My project is important to my client, which means that it is *very* important to me. If I feel that my work is not important to you, I will quickly decide that you are not important to me. Moreover, I gave you a week to complete the project because I figured it would take a week. Now I know that you are going to cram a week's worth of work into two days, further undermining my confidence in the end product. Research takes time, and quality research takes time and care. Partners know this. You need to live it.

Your job is not simply to deliver a memorandum. Your job is to deliver *confidence*. And by waiting to even begin the memo, you have already lost any chance of delivering confidence. You have failed before you have even begun.

Rule Number 8

Finish The Research—
"Almost Done" Is Far From Finished

Research isn't finished until it is finished.

Research has two states: "Finished" and "not finished." There is no in-between. If you are not "finished," then you are "not finished."

Your final memorandum must reflect a state of "finished." Sounds obvious? Well, it's not. Most people operate in a world of "pretty sure" and "I think so." Attorneys are not most people. We live in the world of bedrock certainty. Even when we are uncertain, we are certain about our uncertainty. We know what we know, and we know what we don't know.

This is so because this is what our clients pay us for. We are not paid for speculation, but for answers. We are the backstop, the final safety net, the guarantee. When the client needs an answer they can absolutely and confidently rely on, they call us. What we say will be taken as gospel. Very expensive decisions will be made on the strength of your research memorandum. Act accordingly.

Finish the research, so that you can offer your answer with absolute confidence. When research is "almost" finished (*i.e.,* "not finished"), you are living in the realm of "pretty sure." Shake this habit. You left that world behind when you took the bar exam.

How do you know that the research is finished? Easy— when you have absolute confidence in your answer. If you do not have absolute confidence, then go back until you do.

But do not declare yourself satisfied just because you find the answer. You must not only find the answer, but be certain that it is the final answer and that there are no other answers. The law is not always as straightforward as it seems. It is not unusual for statutes to be interpreted by courts to mean something quite different from what they appear to at first glance.

You must have absolute confidence not only in what you have read, but in what you have not read.

Go to the primary source. It doesn't count until *you* have read it. You have to look at the actual statute, the actual case, the actual contract, the actual correspondence. An email from your client telling you that he executed the contract last month means nothing. You need to see the executed contract yourself. Nothing is real until you touch it.

> A patent infringement dispute hinged on whether the inventor had assigned his rights in the invention to his employer. The employer produced a contract that assigned the rights, but their copy had only been executed by the employer, not by the inventor.
>
> Testimony that the inventor had signed the contract was unpersuasive without an executed contract to show for it, and the court ruled that the inventor owned the patent.
>
> The employer's lawyer was sure that the inventor had signed the contract. Turned out he was actually only pretty sure.

The "primary source" varies depending on the nature of the research, and is not always obvious. Memoranda written by other members of your firm are not primary sources. Legal information pamphlets from other law firms are not primary sources. Anything "discussing" the law is not a primary source. The law itself is the primary source. We all know to get our cases from reputable sources, like WestLaw or physical reporters, but determining what counts as a "primary source" for statutes and regulations can be trickier. Determining whether you have the final contract can be trickier yet. But determine you must.

Secondary sources are great. From treatises to *Restatements* to the internet to your colleague down the hall to existing contract summaries, and all points in between, secondary sources are essential to successful research and you should use them to your advantage. You will often begin your research with secondary sources, to gain general understanding of the issues. You will often end your research with secondary sources, to confirm that there are no known issues that you have not addressed.

But they are *secondary*.

You can begin and end your research with secondary sources, but ultimately your research must rest upon primary sources, for only primary sources give certainty. The purpose of secondary sources is to help you identify and locate all of the relevant primary sources. In the end, if it is not a primary source, it is not a source at all. Secondary sources are nothing more than hearsay.

Once your research is complete, you can finish your memo. At that point, you might discover that your research was not complete after all. This is normal—the process of writing the research down frequently uncovers holes and gaps that were not in your mind when you started. After all, before you started the research you might have had only a passing familiarity with the legal issue—yet the expected result at the end of the research is absolute, watertight certainty. Make sure to budget time to finish the research, then finish the memo, and then finish the research again.

But ultimately you must finish the research, and you must have confidence that you have finished the research. If somebody asks you "are you sure?" you must be able to answer in the affirmative without hesitation and without breaking a sweat.

If you cannot, then you are not finished.

Rule Number 9

Become Bilingual: Learn Legalese

Junior associates usually have a decent grasp of the English language. Many even have English degrees. Unfortunately for them, legal memoranda are not written in English, but in legalese, which is a different language altogether.

Legalese is a language both simple and complex. It is deceptively close to English, and shares a large vocabulary with English. Much like English, legalese has a wide variety of dialects, some of which can barely be recognized as the same language. Memo-legalese is quite different from contract-legalese, which is very different indeed from brief-legalese.

Unlike English, however, you cannot simply stumble by with your own dialect. You must master the correct dialect for your task. And right now that means memo-legalese. Whether you later will have to learn contract-legalese or brief-legalese (or probate-legalese, or patent-legalese) will depend primarily on your chosen practice area. Now, however, you must learn to write memo-legalese, which conveniently is a sort of *lingua franca* of legalese dialects.

At its core, legalese is quite simple. There is one central guiding principle that drives the choice of every word: Be Exact.

Every word, every sentence, every paragraph is there for a purpose, and chosen because it was exactly the right word, sentence, or paragraph to convey your point. There is no fluff in legalese—even what looks like fluff has a purpose and is chosen carefully for a specific reason.

If you can but truly master this principle, you have mastered legalese. All of the other rules in this book dealing with writing (or, indeed, in any legal writing book) are special cases of Be Exact.

Do not just sit down and write. Have a plan. Then turn that plan into something specific. And then choose your sentences and words carefully to fit your specific plan. And then go back and edit to make sure the sentences and words *exactly* fit your specific plan. No random words, no random thoughts, no random cases, no random opinions or observations. No stragglers from prior drafts, no leftover sentences that do not conform.

Once you know what you are trying to say, say exactly that. If your sentence can be misinterpreted or misunderstood, then it is not exact. When writing contract-legalese or brief-legalese, your language has to be so exact that it cannot be misinterpreted even on purpose by readers bent on mischief. When writing memo-legalese you at least have the benefit of a (more or less) sympathetic audience, but do not let this lull you into complacency.

Every sentence, every word. Your writing makes sense to you—after all, you wrote it, and you know what you meant to say. Your readers, however, did not and do not, and probably will not unless you write exactly. Lawyers can agonize for hours over a three-sentence letter, because sometimes that letter is very important and has to convey exactly a particular tone and message. And if so, every word has to be chosen exactly. Even "casual" emails should be subjected to the same level of care. Lawyers do not communicate casually; we communicate exactly. Every sentence, every word. Always.

We had retained local counsel to issue a security opinion for a real estate financing transaction.

The local counsel had an unfortunate habit of referring to the document as the "securities opinion" in conversation, apparently unaware or uncaring of the rather significant difference between the two terms.

The finance partner at our firm was able to restrain himself only until references to the "securities opinion" started showing up in client memos.

You need to write such that the reader has no choice but to go where you wish. If it is a contract, then there should be no doubt as to which obligations belong to whom. If it is a brief, then there should be no doubt that the law and facts necessarily lead to the favorable ruling. If it is a memorandum, then there should be no doubt as to what your conclusions are, and why they are what they are, and—most importantly—that your conclusions are trustworthy. Do not allow sloppy or ambiguous language to let your reader drift away from where you want them to go. Do not give your reader a choice.

Exactitude is your overriding goal. Sacrifice idiom and grammar if needed to preserve exactitude. A pretty turn of phrase may keep the reader engaged, but it is not exact. Clever understatement and amusing similes are not useful in a legal memorandum—not because we don't like humor in our memos (and in fact we do not like humor in our memos)—but because understatements and similes are by definition inexact. Say what the thing actually *is,* not what it is similar to or greater than. Use the exact words to give the exact answer.

In some forms of legalese—most notably brief-legalese—clever language and pretty prose may occasionally be appropriate when used skillfully. This is not the case for memo-legalese. You obviously want (and need) your memo to be easy to comprehend, but your memo is useless (or worse) if it is not exact. Memoranda are not persuasive; they are there to convey information. If it isn't information, don't convey it.

And convey it you must, in painstaking detail. Not only must your memo be exact, but it must be complete. Do not assume that the reader knows what you are talking about, because she won't. You are not sitting next to the partner to explain every passage, so your document must stand on its own.

In everyday English, we frown on using the same words many times in the same sentence, paragraph, or document. In legalese, it is required. If your particular case or contract uses the phrase "right, title, and interest" and this phrase is important, then you must also use that exact and entire phrase in your memo—every time. Seeing "right, title, and interest" four times in a sentence can be headache-inducing to a reader not familiar with legalese, but occasionally short-handing to "right" or "title" or "interest" is confusion-inducing to the legalese reader, which is far worse. You must use full repetition, even when it becomes repetitive. Anything less is not exact. The reader will not know whether you used "title" instead of "right, title, and interest" purely as a convenient abbreviation or because you were highlighting a difference. Only you will know whether you used the correct word or not.

Words are free—use as many as you need.

To succeed at memo-writing, you absolutely must maintain full control over each word in the memorandum. Be literal. Be repetitive if required. But above all, be exact.

Rule Number 10

Don't Give Me A Headache

Because of the central importance of exactitude, legalese can occasionally be difficult to read. Sometimes this is not so important (like with the small print on your credit card application), but other times it can be a fatal flaw. One of those times is when you are writing a legal memorandum.

The purpose of a legal memorandum is to convey information. If your memo is so dense and convoluted, or confusing and disorganized, that the reader cannot understand it, or is simply disinclined to even read it, then you have failed. Without sacrificing exactness, you must present information in a readable format, and without giving me a headache when I read it.

Memos written by summer associates and junior associates are notoriously headache-inducing. Many partners simply refuse to work with summer associates and junior associates, in part because of the high likelihood of a headache. Even those of us who do regularly work with the rookies approach each new memo with a sense of dread and foreboding.

You should strive to write memos that will not give me a headache—memos that will make me want to ask you to write another, because the memo you just wrote was so easy to read. This is a skill you can and should master. Luckily, you have tools at your disposal.

Definitions are your friends. While you cannot use defined terms as liberally in a memo as you can in a contract, they are available to you, and you should take advantage. Do not type out "that certain Memorandum of Understanding, dated as of January 25, 2008, between Bank of America, N.A., and George's Lumber Supply, Inc." every time it comes up in your memo evaluating that document. That is guaranteed to give me a headache. Instead, define it as the "MOU." Importantly, you are not doing this to make the memo shorter but to make it more readable. The full name of the MOU is not an important part of the discussion, and thus nothing is lost by not repeating in full.

You cannot abbreviate randomly in the memo, however, because then I will wonder whether we are talking about the same memorandum of understanding. You need to say it once to be exact about what the "MOU" is, but once that is established there is no need to repeat. Define all major parties and documents along the same lines. And then, once you have defined those terms, stick to them. Use the defined term for every instance of that phrase, not just some of the time: once you have defined "MOU" do not suddenly refer to the "Memorandum." Stick to your terms.

You also cannot casually define important phrases like "right, title, and interest" as "RTI" (or anything else, for that matter). The reason you keep repeating "right, title, and interest" in full is because each of those words have importance to the point you are making. Definitions create a label for a known thing, they do not simply abbreviate frequent phrases. The definitions are there for me, not you. They are there to make the memorandum easier to read, not just to save you from extra typing.

Similarly, your definitions must make sense, and should preferably be standard. "MOU," for instance, is a standard abbreviation, and therefore a standard definition, for "Memorandum of Understanding." Defining it as the "MemUnd" would be functional, but you would be the odd one out with your strange definition, which would mark you as a rookie. More importantly, it would be a distraction for the reader accustomed to a different definition, and would give me a headache. How could you know that the normal definition was "MOU?" Well, you probably couldn't, initially. But when you have been corrected once, pay attention and learn. And if you paid attention to Rule #5—Understand the Facts—and therefore read the relevant documents in the file, chances are good that you found numerous other documents referring to the "MOU" and none referring to the "MemUnd," which should tell you everything you need to know about how to define this document.

Other definitions are easier to figure out. Avoid defined terms that are confusingly similar or unnecessarily complex, or that imply an incorrect meaning. Defined terms that are pronounceable make discussions easier. The "Bank" or "BofA" are better definitions for "Bank of America, N.A." than "BOANA"—unless, of course, there are numerous other banks involved, or other Bank of America entities with similar names. Definitions should be intuitive and simple without being misleading. In most cases, you will follow convention. This means that you read what has been written before, and follow it: look for how terms have been defined in other documents in your case or transaction, and use those same terms and definitions.

Use subdivisions and headings. Divide your memorandum into manageable sections. Headings provide both a break in the text and a glimpse into the future. Subdivisions and headings make your dense brick of legal reasoning easier to read. Numerals are helpful, even essential. Numbered and lettered headings convey a sense of progress. Did you notice how this book consists of short chapters with numbered descriptive headings? If your memo is long enough, you might even consider a table of contents.

Having the correct subdivisions and headings not only makes the memorandum easier to read, but helps you organize your thoughts and conclusions. Organizing the memo will help you sharpen your analysis. It is easy to get bogged down in your own mental maze of cases and contracts, and a well-organized and subdivided memorandum will help you accomplish a memo that is not only easy to read but also more exact.

Be careful with pronouns and inexact references. Using the proper name of entities and documents instead of pronouns reduces the potential for headache-inducing confusion, and if you use your definitions carefully, not much readability will be sacrificed. Your English professor might frown upon multiple uses of "MOU" in a single sentence without replacing any reference with "it," "that," or even "the document," but your partner will thank you (or at least not complain). If I have to spend even three seconds deciphering whether "it" refers to the Bank or to the Borrower, I will feel that headache creeping in.

> I asked a summer associate to analyze and evaluate a rather complex stack of corporate documents and loan documents in a messy financing, and to research the law on some of the sticking points.
>
> The memo was very, very thorough. It was also very, very long, and completely void of any subsections or headings (beyond the minimalist "Discussion" and "Conclusion" macro-sections).
>
> I gave up trying to read it, took some Advil, and asked the summer associate to reorganize.

Use standard formatting. Yes, it does not "matter" substantively whether you use half-inch or full-inch margins, or an 11-point or 12-point typeface. The memo will still contain the same analysis. Use standard formatting anyway. I read legal documents, including memos, day in and day out, and have done so for many years. Most of them use more or less the same formatting. If your memo does not, then you just gave me a headache. I will spend precious seconds and minutes wondering why your header is different, why your font is different, why your margins are different from all those other memos I have read. And I will be distracted by these differences, which will interfere with your ability to convey information.

You want everything except the content to fade away and become invisible. You do not want me to notice the typeface, the margins, or the formatting. You want me to focus on one thing alone, and that is your brilliant analysis. Even if you think an 11-point font is "better" than a 12-point font, that does not matter. If the firm's standard is 12-point, then your standard is 12-point.

Do not create distractions. If it is not important, make it invisible.

Fortunately, this is usually pretty easy. Most firms have standardized templates for common documents, including memoranda. Use the firm template, and do not deviate unless there is a very good reason to do so. Do not switch the typeface just because you prefer Courier over Times New Roman. Do not switch the places for "Date" and "Re:" in the header because that is how your legal writing instructor said memos should look.

There is exactly ONE way that memos should look, and it is the way that will make me not think about (or even notice) how the memo looks, and will therefore not give me a headache. Be thankful that the firm provides these templates to you, so that you need spend no time worrying about typefaces, font size, margins, or any of that. Instead, you can spend your time doing actual work, and you can do so without giving me a headache. Use the firm template.

Your job when writing is to convey information. To do so you must write the exact information you intend to convey, and you must write it in such a way that it will actually be read, sans headache.

Rule Number 11
Citations—Not Just For Bluebooks Anymore

All through high school, college, and law school, your teachers and professors were harping on you about citation format. APA style. MLA style. Chicago style. Like an ancient ritual of adulthood, you had to show your mastery of these arcane quasilanguages to pass before the Altar of Higher Learning. Similarly, no paper was complete without a long list of impressive-looking references that you had (allegedly) consulted for your research paper, one in a procession of seemingly pointless bibliographies and citation procedures imposed upon you for the sadistic amusement of ivory-tower professors.

You can forget all about that now.

You can no longer dismiss citation formatting as a pointless exercise. Proper use of sources and proper citation-formatting are now for real, and they are important.

Your memorandum exists to convey information. While part of the information being conveyed consists of your thoughts and opinions, the real substance and foundation of the memorandum is the information you gleaned from the underlying sources. Underlying primary sources. Underlying high-quality current primary sources. This is not an essay or novella. The statutes, the cases, the contracts, the regulations...*those* are what the memorandum is really about. That is what I am looking for when reading your memo. I want—*need*—analysis, for sure, but not in a vacuum. I want to know exactly what you were insightfully analyzing.

A simple conclusion that "the law is *x*" is handy, and may allow me to take immediate action. But when we really get into it, it is the research and analysis of your memo that is important. This is the part that gets incorporated into the brief, that lays the foundation for contract revisions and changed corporate policy. This is the part that will be read carefully to help us navigate the minefield of the law. But while this is important, your memorandum is *not* the law.

At some point somebody is going to look up the statutes, contracts, cases, or regulations underlying your memorandum. And this means a couple of things for you:

First major point: Correct and proper citation. An outright incorrect citation will lead the reader to the wrong source, which is very bad. Remember Rule #1—Proofread, and proofread again. You must proofread your citations, just as thoroughly as you proofread everything else. Do not skim over the citations when proofreading. Check to make sure the section references and page references are correct. Be sure that for each cite you are including a pinpoint cite—a citation to the exact page where you are drawing your information. If you cannot include a pinpoint cite, chances are it is a source that should not be in your memo.

Even if the substance of the citation is correct—the proper Reporter, volume, page and pinpoint cites, year, and so on—incorrect format will cause problems. Appearance is important. You may not care that you italicized the wrong part of the citation. To the partner, however, this counts the same as any other typo—it is proof of your inability or unwillingness to make the document perfect. Incorrect citation formatting does not say "I don't care if my italicizing conforms with Bluebook standards, because the substance of my work is good." It simply says "I don't care."

Non-standard citation formatting falls under Rule #10—Don't Give Me A Headache. If everybody italicizes one way and you do it differently, it slows down the reading—my reading—thereby hindering your mission of conveying information. To lawyers who read many, many citations every day, failure to conform to standard citation format is just as jarring as misusing "their" and "there." It distracts from the point you are trying to make, and it casts a shadow of doubt over every other aspect of your work. Like other aspects of your work that may appear to be "only" style, citation is not merely stylistic—it goes directly to the substance of your work, to what it means to have lawyerly skill. As with odd formatting, non-standard citation is a distraction, and is thus wrong.

> A mid-level associate asked a junior associate to research a difficult tax issue in a complex financing transaction.
>
> The junior associate, after extensive research, produced an in-depth and lengthy memorandum. To assist the reader, he attached all of the numerous sources in a giant .pdf file. Instead of using normal citations to case reporters, however, the junior associate cited to the cases based on their location within the .pdf file.
>
> The mid-level associate did not find this particularly helpful. Instead, he got a headache.

Moreover, if your citation errors are non-obvious (which they often are), they will be circulated widely and perhaps duplicated. Legal memos often form the basis for other documents, sometimes years later. Pieces of your document could be incorporated into client letters or presentations. Your formatting errors could end up in a brief, where judicial clerks will take a very dim view indeed of your departure from norm.

Don't do it.

Citation formatting and accuracy is no longer just a formality. Take it seriously. Think about who will be reading what you write. Partners and judicial clerks were often the ones who instructed new law review members in Bluebook citation, way back when. They *know* proper citation, and they know why it is important. They care, and so should you.

Second major point: read your sources. This sounds shockingly obvious. After all, how could you have completed the research—or even reached the middle of your research—without having read the sources? The answer, of course, is that it happens all the time. This is not so much a matter of outright fraud as it is simple laziness.

One ever-popular approach is to turn an indirect citation into a direct citation. You read an article or a case that quotes another case that seems particularly relevant. So you cite the quoted case. STOP. Did you read the case you just cited? No? Then you ought not be citing it. This is not a mere technicality—the ultimate truth is that YOU are responsible for the content of your cited materials. Maybe the article you read misquoted, or took the quote out of context, or was itself a lazy taking from yet another source. Maybe there is simply an error in the reference, and an attempt to look up the case will fail. Either way, you are responsible. Nothing is real until you read it yourself. The "it" is the primary source. The actual case, the actual contract, right in front of your eyes.

Shortcuts like these are common in college. Do not do this even once in the real world. In college, an impressive list of references might contribute to your "A" grade, even if half of the listed references were irrelevant sources that you had never actually consulted. That type of paper-padding ended upon your graduation. *These* readers will actually read your sources—especially if it's something that doesn't seem quite right, or something that raises a flag or issue that might be central to the case (but which you, of course, do not know). Your readers will not look at your list of citations and declare themselves satisfied—many will instead look up each individual case and section cited. If your sources do not say exactly what you have declared that they do, *you* have a problem.

Your readers will not review your sources to "check your work." Your readers are not professors, and they are not grading you. They want the answer. Your readers will check your sources because they care about the content. They will check the sources to further educate themselves on the subject matter. For many readers, your memorandum is merely the beginning of *their* learning process. You have provided the road map, and they intend to follow it. We are lawyers—we will turn every stone, for that is what we do. We are also curious, and if you have noted something of interest, or followed a line of argument we find useful, surprising, or questionable, we will likely pursue it, sometimes just to confirm our own understanding of the law.

Therefore, your citations and sources must be absolutely correct and accurate—each and every one, down to the letter, italics, and parentheses. Read and confirmed, verbatim, by you. Citations are not there to show off—they are there for the very reason the Bluebook exists: to point your readers directly and without fuss to the source. "Direct" means accurate, both in location and in context. "Without fuss" means legal citation in compliance with Bluebook style. "The source" means the real source. The primary source.

For many attorneys, the internet is a popular research tool. This is good—the internet is immensely powerful. What is not good is citing a website as a source, no matter how reliable it may be. This should only be done as a last resort. Citing a URL does not always provide meaningful information about the nature of the source, making it difficult for the reader to gauge its reliability without investigation or a clear line of authority. If you must cite a URL, include a parenthetical explaining your cite, and be prepared to address why that website is the *best* source.

Websites are also transitory—a URL citation to a news story on Reuter's website, for instance, might not be valid when the memo is read, and almost certainly will not be valid when the memo is read again five years later. A citation to that same story in a printed newspaper will always be correct, even if it is more difficult to locate. Of course, you will have printed or saved copies, so it will not be difficult for you to locate if needed, but your readers will not have that benefit.

Websites can blur the line between primary and secondary sources. A citation to a website containing a statute may look like a primary source (a statute), but in fact it is not. The primary source is the statute itself, not the website, and it is the statute that should be cited. The same goes for cases and all other primary sources.

Lastly, consider whether to attach copies of your sources. If your reader intends to review the sources anyway, you will do him a service by actually providing copies. When to attach sources? It is a decision for you to make. Some partners always want sources attached, others never want them attached. An easy way to start is simply to ask the partner whether he wants to see the sources or not. Many partners actually prefer to see your marked-up and highlighted copies of the source materials, and few will object if you have them handy.

Sometimes it is relatively obvious whether sources ought to be attached. If your memorandum summarizes two boxes of contracts, you probably should not attach the contracts. If your memorandum rests entirely on three seminal cases, you almost certainly should attach those three cases. Other times it is less obvious, as when you are applying a statute to a contract. You would probably attach the statute, and maybe the contract, but perhaps not all of the interpretive caselaw. Ultimately it is up to you to decide, for it is your memorandum and your responsibility.

This decision, as with all other memorandum-related decisions, should be guided by one central principle: Be helpful. A memorandum is a tool, a means to an end. If convention must be bent to be helpful, then bend convention. Your goal is not to slavishly follow set precepts, but to advance the purpose of the partner and the interests of the client.

Rule Number 12
Know When To Quote 'Em, Know When To Not

Everybody loves a good quote. People start speeches with them, end speeches with them, intersperse them throughout their papers in high school and college, and toss them about in social conversation.

Summer associates and junior associates often embrace their love for quotes, and it shows. Sometimes this is well and good. Other times, frankly, you just need to stop with the quoting already. All too often, memos are either simply a collection of neatly organized quotes or completely devoid of specifics that desperately needed to be quoted. Neither is acceptable.

This is an area where you truly need to apply Rule #4— Understand The Context. Quotes are either essential for specificity or legal weight and therefore absolutely required, or they are useless, unnecessary, and distracting. If your quote is required, quote. Otherwise, don't.

Memoranda written in the context of a lawsuit should often quote judicial opinions liberally. This is because memos written during litigation often end up being used wholesale in briefs, where quoting judicial opinions is necessary and appropriate. If not actually copied into the brief, a litigation memo will often form the foundation for the drafting of the brief. Either way, the weight of specific judicial reasoning and language is important.

Memoranda written in a transactional context, on the other hand, should generally quote judicial opinions quite sparingly. This is because transactional memos will most likely not be incorporated into a brief or be used to develop a brief, but will instead be used to develop litigation-avoidance strategies.

Statutes and regulation should often be quoted in both litigation and non-litigation contexts. Interpretation of statute or regulation frequently rests on a single word or phrase, and analysis should always be done with the actual statute or regulation. The same goes for contracts. Quote the contract language in question when undertaking thorough analysis. When interpreting statutes, regulations, and contracts, the specific wording can be crucial: the presence or absence of a single word—and sometimes a comma—can be the deciding factor in determining the outcome.

When you quote, you quote. Paraphrasing is different from quoting. You can tweak a paraphrase, but never a quote. To the contrary, you must be absolutely certain that you are quoting the source exactly correctly. Not just every word, but every character in every word, and every comma and every period. Many times a peculiarity in the original won't matter—but sometimes it will. And when that sometimes happens you absolutely must have the exactly correct version in your memo.

This, of course, applies not just to quoting, but to your entire memo (and indeed to the entire practice of law): perfect means perfect. Not just facts, law, context, citation style, and quotes, but every single character that results from every single keystroke you make. The standard for your entire memo is, and should be, perfect. If it isn't perfect, it isn't finished.

Quotes are a necessary part of almost any legal memorandum. Memos are not essays, but evaluations of underlying sources. Failing to quote when necessary is a significant error. But at the same time, excessive or unnecessary quoting is misleading and distracting. If there is a specific reason to quote—then quote. If there isn't—don't. If your memo is headed for a brief, or if there is a particular holding that is carefully stated and central to your memorandum, quote away. Otherwise, think twice.

This does not mean that you can quote with abandon when working on a lawsuit. Not at all. It means simply that you will encounter more quotable (and therefore quote-required) language when doing litigation research than when you are reviewing caselaw in a transactional context.

In college, you often shaped your papers around the good quotes. You cannot do that anymore. Quoting is a tool available to you, but a tool that should be used with great care and deliberation. In no event should the quotes be a driving force in the drafting process.

> A summer associate was reviewing and evaluating a joint venture agreement for me to determine whether a breach had occurred.
>
> While his memo discussed the applicable provisions of the agreement at length, and included the appropriate section references, the memo did not quote the actual agreement—not even once.
>
> Given that the conclusion depended entirely on a few specific words in the agreement, the memo had to be redone, and I had a headache.

When you do quote, keep it small. Block quotes, while they look cool on the page, are essentially code for "skip me." Nothing will get less attention in your memorandum than a huge block quote. Large block quotes do not look important; they look detached and unrelated. They are distractions that tend to get overlooked. If you must include a block quote, consider adding emphasis to the most important language within the quote, to help focus the reader's attention where it matters.

Quote the sentence, phrase, or word that is the center of the discussion. Quote the part that is needed, that is helpful. Litigation memos, and memos dealing with contracts and statutes (or regulations) can often end up—correctly—being full of quotes. Fine. But make the quotes the absolute essence of what is needed. Use ellipses to focus on the relevant parts. Cut out irrelevant subsections or dicta. Do not simply quote an entire indemnification provision. This is not helpful. If the entire section is needed as a reference, then include it as an attachment, but do not plunk the whole thing in the middle of the text. Quote the essential parts; attach the rest.

Even in a quote-heavy context, be selective. Your memo may need to quote several holdings on the issue at hand, but there is no need to include quotes from each case in your jurisdictional string-cite (unless the issue at hand is jurisdiction, of course). Cases are quoted when they are important, and when the specific language is important. When citing several cases that say essentially the same thing, it is generally not necessary to quote each one.

The purpose of the memorandum is to be helpful. Every part of the memo should contribute to that goal. If the quote is helpful only in its exact form, use it. If the quote will help make a better brief, use it. If the quote contains specific important words, use it. If the quote is not useful, do not use it. If the quote is harmless and useless but clever and insightful, do not use it. If the quote can be paraphrased into your memo without losing value, do not use it. If you want to use the quote because the case is obscure and impressive, do not use it.

Be helpful. Include all helpful and required quotes, but do not unnecessarily burden your memo with clumsy intrusions from other writers. Legal memoranda are hard enough to read as it is, especially when written by summer associates. Don't make it worse than it has to be.

Rule Number 13

Cut The Fluff

Research can be fun. It's true—it really can be fun. It can be a challenge, a treasure hunt, a logic-building exercise, a wonderful learning experience. When done right, research can be deeply rewarding.

The catch is that it is only fun for the person actually doing it. I asked you to do some research. I am glad you are having a good time, but that does not mean that I want a blow-by-blow. This is not a novel. I do not need or want to hear about all the interesting things you discovered on your path to the answer. I just want the answer. More precisely, I want *just* the answer. Please just give me my answer.

Legal researchers sometimes get carried away, and can't help but share all the things they discovered on their quest. This type of memo, the Research Notes Memo, is often characterized by excessive and disjointed quoting. These memoranda read like a sequential retelling of your research adventure: "This case says 'x,' and then this case says 'y,' but then I found a case that says 'z,' and then I knew that the first two cases were irrelevant, oh and here is a case that says something else entirely." I want your summary, your analysis, your conclusion. I do not want to relive the last week of your life. I have a job to do too.

You might come across interesting cases, which might have interesting fact patterns, illustrating particularly interesting legal points. That's great. But if they do not relate to the answer to my question, I don't want to read about it in the memo. Old cases that were overruled but are historically interesting? Don't want them. This is not a thesis on the legal history of my question. I just want the answer to my current question.

I understand that you want to share. I really do. But a legal memo is not there for your enjoyment, or mine. It is there to present focused information: a specific question for a specific client in a specific situation. Including a juicy case that you think I will enjoy is nice, but incorrect. If it is not relevant and on point, do not include it.

> As a junior associate I was researching a point of law under the Fair Debt Collection Practices Act.
>
> I came across a case where the court with great gusto and eloquence declared that the defendant's collection method of barging into debtors' homes in the night while wielding two nickel-plated pistols was in fact not permitted under the law.
>
> The case was not relevant to my memo, but I couldn't resist the amusing facts, and found a way to include it anyway.
>
> The partner promptly agreed that it was funny, and just as quickly struck it out.

It can be tempting to squeeze all of your research into the memo. This is a mistake. Yes, I understand that you worked very hard to uncover all these cases. Yes, I understand that you don't want to "waste" good research. But that does not mean that every case you found has to be included. Jamming every last bit of data you found into the memo is a common junior associate mistake, and one that will give me a headache.

You do not get points based on volume. You get points based on successful transmittal of the required information. Sometimes great scenes get cut from movies, and for good reason. Sometimes the director can obsess over whether a scene gets deleted. No matter. If it needs to be cut, it needs to be cut. The same applies here. It does not matter how great the case is—if it has to go, it has to go. If it is relevant to my question, it stays. If it isn't, it goes. Do not become enamored with your brilliant analysis of the irrelevant.

Similarly, stay on topic. Astonishingly, summer associates frequently feel the need to include in their memos a discussion of "something else I found interesting." This might be a related legal issue that captured your imagination, or simply a detailed discussion of all seventeen exceptions to the statute, even though only four are relevant to our case. In either event, it does not belong in the memo.

Along the same lines, associates sometimes like to include editorials regarding their own views on the law. This is fluff. I understand that you disapprove of the law, and think that the judge made a horrible decision. I understand it, I might even agree—I just don't care. It is not relevant to my client, and thus it is not relevant to me.

Stay on topic. Anything that is not required in the memo is extraneous and should be excluded. There are no optional parts to a memo. Every sentence, every word—chosen for a reason. If it is not required, it does not belong: it is fluff, and needs to be cut.

Rule Number 14

Impress Mr. Spock

Rule #9—Become Bilingual: Learn Legalese—requires that you be exact in your writing. Of equal importance to being exact in your writing is being exact in your thinking. Summer associate memos meander. And then meander some more. They meander not because of poor writing, but because of poor thinking.

Yes, I know you are smart. We all are. That's not the problem. The problem is that in school few of us learn, let alone are taught, the logical precision that is required for success as an attorney. If your undergraduate degree is in logic, mathematics, or computer science, you have a sense of this aspect of the law. Yet those disciplines cheat by using "languages" (symbols) that are inherently and necessarily precise, and in those disciplines the need for precision is obvious. The written and especially spoken word is not precise, however, and neither is much of our thinking. A majority of new lawyers have not taken undergraduate degrees in mathematics or a hard science, and are thus uncomfortable with the tension between language as they have known it and language as they must relearn it to be effective lawyers.

You must force your thoughts to be as precise as a mathematical formula. This is true for the entire practice of law, not just memoranda. But the legal memo in particular gives the neophyte attorney ample opportunity fail at this central requirement. You will not be able to write a clear memorandum unless you have clear thoughts to transcribe.

You have heard the phrase "thinking like a lawyer" repeatedly, of course. Preparing a legal memorandum is a large part of what *thinking like a lawyer* actually means. In a sense it is the culmination of your law school years, and the beginning of your law practice expertise.

You must be a mathematician, a scientist, a logician. Yet instead of endless formulae or hypotheticals or black letter law, you must now apply the same rigor to all that you learned in law school (and to that larger body of knowledge you will gain in your research); to the facts surrounding the client's case; to the words needed to put those two together. That, however, is just the start. A memo is not like a law exam where you regurgitate black letter law in a rushed and haphazard attempt to wow a professor. It is nearly the opposite, as there are no limits as to which doctrines might be applicable, which cases might be of sudden importance, which regulations might upset a prior line of thinking. Nothing is predetermined in a memo. And your goal is not to impress; it is to answer a specific, finite legal question drawing upon *all* of the law.

That is the proverbial "thinking like a lawyer." And that is how you must approach your job. You are a logician who works with law and facts, with a machine-like insistence on precision. Answering a legal question like a politician or a salesman will lead to disaster.

This is a central bedrock principle of the profession.

Nothing—*nothing*—in this book, or in any aspect of the practice of law, will be meaningful or successful unless and until you master rigorous thought.

> Over the years I have seen summer associates and junior associates write memoranda that contradict themselves, have unsupported conclusions, fail to state obvious conclusions, fail to prove premises, have premises that do not lead to the conclusion, have premises that led nowhere, and generally fail to reflect organized, rigorous thought.
>
> Many are now successful attorneys who look back on their early efforts…and wince.

It is easy to think that your task is to write a memo, and to research what you need to write the memo. The opposite is true.

Your task is to do the research, and write the resultant memo. The memo does not drive the research; the research drives the memo. Apply rigorous thought to the research and the writing will follow. Attempting to squeeze logic into what you want to write leads to failure.

How to do this?

Organize every thought. For every thought, for every fact, for every law, for every conclusion, ask "why?" and "then what?" Is the fact true? If this fact is true, then what? And why? Why is it important? Does this exception apply? Why not? If not, then what other exceptions do apply? No fact or law just *is*. There is always a "why" and "then what"...followed by another "why" and "then what." No statement is obvious. "You know what I mean" is not in our vocabulary.

You research the facts and the law to reach the conclusion. Your facts and law must support that conclusion. Moreover, they must not support any other conclusion. If you tell me that A and B lead to C, you need to be able to explain to me why A and B do not also lead to D. If both C and D are possible conclusions, then you either need to do more research to determine the correct conclusion, or conclude that both are correct conclusions. You also have to explain why E is not a correct conclusion.

Above all, the key to logical thought is organized thought. You must be able to parse the facts, to identify individual facts and laws and the relationships among them all, and not just see a muddle of information. Run through "if-then" exercises. List out the parties, the rules, the principal facts. Graphic representations can be helpful, as can a hand-drawn flowchart showing the relationships among the various parties and documents.

But by whatever means, you must wrap your logical arms around the problem before you even think about writing.

Rule Number 15

Write For Your Audience, Not For Yourself

Somebody is going to read your memo. If it is good, many people will read your memo. Different readers have different needs and wants, and you need to write to the correct readers.

Write your memo for your actual reader, not some theoretical reader. Ask yourself who is the true target audience for your memo. Sure, the partner will read the memo, but is he the true target? Is this memo intended for the client? If so, will it go to the client's in-house lawyer, or the CFO, or an engineer? Is it going to opposing counsel?

Is the reader clamoring to read this memo, or will it merely be one of many papers across her desk that day? Does the reader have a legal, technical, or financial background, or none of the above? Is the reader sophisticated? Is he familiar with the transaction or case? Is your client the lender or the borrower in the transaction? The plaintiff or the defendant? Is the reader the main person on the case, or the supervisor? Might the memo end up as evidence in court?

Each of these questions must be asked and answered by you before you can start—much less, finish—your memo. These questions shape not just the approach you take to the writing, but the approach you take to the research. Your job is to convey information, so you must present the information in a fashion that fits the reader. You cannot write in a vacuum—you must know who will be reading the memo, and write accordingly.

A client memo, for instance, might take a gentler tone when evaluating strategic options or past mistakes than an internal memo. If your memo will be read by accountants, you will need to simplify the legal analysis, but can include all the numbers you want. If the memo is intended for a senior executive, extra care should be given to an up-front summary, as very possibly nothing past the first page will be read. Executives almost universally read only the Executive Summary—or just the first and last paragraphs of the Executive Summary—before jumping ahead to whatever specific issue they are concerned about, if indeed they read any more at all. If the memo is for the deal workhorse, however, the up-front summary is merely an introduction, and the in-depth analysis is the focus.

Concepts like "detrimental reliance" and *"stare decisis"* will need some explanation if discussed for a non-lawyer, and may even merit some extra substantive discussion if the memo will be read by non-litigators. If the reader is not familiar with the industry involved in the case or transaction, jargon should be used sparingly, and it should be defined or explained. On the other hand, for insiders jargon can be a powerful tool for conveying information, and unnecessary detail and explanation will be annoying or insulting.

> I asked a junior associate to write a memo for a client describing the basic principles and rules of non-utility power plant regulation. The memo was intended as a primer for engineers.
>
> The summer associate drafted an elaborate memorandum describing with great accuracy and detail all of the major rules and regulations. The memo was meticulously footnoted, with detailed citations to back up every statement made.
>
> It was also completely indecipherable to anyone who was not a regulatory attorney.

In the first instance, all of your memos are "for the partner." Many memos, however, do not stop there, and so you also need to know where the memo will ultimately end up. If you are a tax lawyer, many of your memos will end up in the hands of corporate lawyers who will not recognize Internal Revenue Code references, and explanation is required. If the memo will never leave the tax department, those explanations may be fluff that needs to be cut.

If possible, you need to understand not just the hat worn by the reader, but also the individual person and his or her personality. Some readers demand short and to-the-point memoranda, others prefer slow and deliberate reasoning.

How to know which approach is correct? Well, figuring that out is a central part of your job. As attorneys, our job is not merely to give people what they ask for, but to give them what they really need, and to give it to them in the format that is the most useful—to them.

This is a skill you will learn through practice, but only if you make it an immediate priority to ask yourself: "who is my reader?" You cannot write a memorandum for the "reasonable man," and you absolutely should not write it in the way *you* would like it. You must be as effective as possible in conveying information, and to do that you must consider the recipient. This recipient is not an amorphous and generic "they"; your reader is a specific someone.

Rule Number 16

Take A Stand

We are not philosophers. We are not research librarians. We are not scientists. We are not politicians. We are not film critics. We sometimes like to pretend to be all of those things, and more. But professionally, we are something else entirely.

We are attorneys.

We are lawyers, counselors, barristers, and solicitors. We are *consiglieri*. And in that capacity, we have one central function: we advise.

We do not merely provide information to our clients. We are not simple information collators. We do not merely present the facts and encourage everybody else to make up their own minds. We do not play all sides of an issue. We advise our clients on what we believe, in our professional opinion, to be the best course of action for them. We are the village wise man, the clever analyst, the vizier. We help our clients sort through the mess to arrive at the correct conclusion. Our clients come to us for advice, not a book report. This is what we do; this is who we are. We *advise*.

Our clients may choose to ignore that advice, and they often will, but they will do so knowing that they have received advice, not just neutrally presented options for their selection.

Write your memo accordingly.

Do not just present the information. Present the information, and based on that information, your intelligent analysis, and your professional experience, present the conclusion.

Most importantly, reach a conclusion.

Many junior associates are afraid to state conclusions. Summer associates even more so. Instead, they timidly dance around the subject, presenting various arguments for or against this conclusion or the other. This, of course, is rewarded in law school and on law exams.

In law practice, this is no good.

You are the one who has reviewed all the cases, the contracts, the documents, the correspondence. You are the one who has compared and contrasted and evaluated. You are the one who is in the best position to reach a conclusion. You. Not me. You.

So do so. Take a stand.

You are going to have to stick your neck out there. Put down in writing what you think the cases *mean*. Declare on the record what the best course of action is. You are not allowed to punt. Tell me what the law *is*, not what it might be. I already knew what the law might be—I can guess as well as you. I want you to tell me what the law *is*.

> A partner asked a summer associate to draft a memo evaluating a particular point of law for a contract negotiation.
>
> The summer associate produced not one, not two, but *three* complete memos—each memo reaching a different conclusion. The summer associate then asked which conclusion the partner wanted to reach.

Your conclusion may be strong or weak, depending on the results of your research. You do not have to declare absolute truth in every memo. But doing the functional equivalent of "you figure it out" is not helpful. You are ATTORNEY. Let me hear you roar. You get paid to reach conclusions. So lay some conclusions on me.

Yes, there will be memos that actually *are* simple summaries or reports, where no conclusion is required or appropriate. And in those cases you should not artificially create an unwanted conclusion. But if you are asked to research something, that almost always means conclusion, whether a conclusion was specifically requested or not.

Importantly, however, reaching a legal or factual conclusion in a memo does not necessarily mean that you reach a conclu-

sion about the resulting course of action. The appropriate conclusion in a research memo will often simply be "the law is x,"
stopping shy of "the client should do y." But that legal conclusion lays the foundation for the actual advice that will be given,
and you must therefore reach an actual legal conclusion. Advice
based on "arguments can be made for and against this interpretation" is not useful advice.

> As a junior associate, I had just finished what I believed to be
> a good contract evaluation memo for a partner, and I was dis-
> cussing the memo in his office.
>
> The partner asked me what I thought the best course of
> action was. I gave a carefully qualified answer, which I
> thought was appropriately "lawyerly."
>
> The partner was not satisfied, and asked me again what
> I thought the client should do. I gave an even more carefully
> qualified answer, taking care not to actually commit to any
> single position, but instead laying out the pros and cons for
> each option.
>
> Now out of patience, the partner looked me in the eye,
> and pointedly asked: "So what is your advice, *counselor?*"

Your conclusion must be well-founded, and backed up by
the logic and discussion in your memorandum. "I think the law
is x" or "I think we should do z" are not useful conclusions.

"Based on the above research, it is highly unlikely that this
claim will succeed" is a useful conclusion, assuming that you
can, and do, back that up. If there are arguments for a different
conclusion, you should address those as well, and explain why
your conclusion is still the correct one.

Offer conclusions and advice—but not decisions. You are
not the client. The client will decide the course of action, not
you. But I will present the options to the client, based upon and
along with your well-founded conclusions regarding the relative
merit of those conclusions. "Option X is the best choice" is

hardly ever good advice—that is simply placing yourself in the shoes of your client. "Option X is most likely to succeed" is subtly different, yet vastly better.

But be careful.

Reaching a conclusion means that you could be wrong. You are not allowed to be wrong, so you should make sure that your conclusion is correct...before you make it. Thus, do not make a conclusion that you cannot back up. Sometimes a conclusion of ignorance is the correct conclusion—and that is fine, so long as you can back up that ignorance with thorough research.

You are allowed to use "weasel words" to qualify your conclusion, so long as those weasel words are justified and appropriate. "Probably" and "maybe" are not appropriate qualifiers to cover up unfinished research. They are appropriate—and required—qualifiers to express the actual state of the law, with associated, precise explanation.

You should not overstate your conclusion—if the result is uncertain, state that the result is uncertain, and state why. Do not err on the side of confidence, or on the side of uncertainty. Do not err at all.

Rule Number 17

Put A Bow On It

So you took care to understand the question, the real question, the facts, the context, the timeline, and the reader. You finished your research, you wrote exactly, using the correct and helpful subdivisions and citations, and you even reached a logical conclusion.

Yet your memo *still* does not meet with partner approval.

What else could you possibly do to make the partner happy? Well, simply put, you have to tie it all together. The memo cannot simply be a collection of individually correct elements. It needs to be a single, perfect entity.

Read your memo. Read it like you never saw it before. (This is another benefit to observing Rule #7—Get On With It Already: the time to let your memo sit before the final, crucial read). Do you know what the memo is about? Is this clear from the first page? Does the memo take you logically from each paragraph to the next? Do you know why there was just another section heading? Are you wondering why *Jones v. Smith* is suddenly presented?

All too often, memoranda written by summer associates and junior associates are disjointed. Each section or even paragraph appears to have been researched and written on a different day. All the elements of logical argument might be there, but not in a logical, coherent order. Discussions of important cases will suddenly appear, without any explanation of what makes them important. Conclusions are stated without any apparent connection to the premises, and sometimes not even to the most basic authorities cited.

Your memo must be wrapped up nice and tight.

Read the memo carefully. Stop after each sentence. Ask yourself what you are thinking now. Did that sentence follow logically from the prior sentence? Did the sentence perhaps raise a question in your mind? If so, was that question answered in the very next sentence? If not, why not?

> I had asked a junior associate to research a highly technical energy regulatory matter for me.
>
> The resulting memorandum was generally excellent, and reached the conclusion I was hoping for with a convincing amount of authority behind it.
>
> Early on, however, the memo quoted a regulation that appeared to go directly against the conclusion, which made me concerned about whether the conclusion was correct, despite the volume of supporting evidence that followed.
>
> This regulation had been interpreted favorably for us in a subsequent case, but this was not explained in the memo, leaving me to wonder.
>
> As a result, I had to waste time getting an explanation from the associate—an explanation that should have been in the memo to begin with—and the memo had to be revised before I could send it to the client.

When you arrive to a conclusion, was that conclusion logical, or did it take you by surprise? Did you see it coming, or are you wondering how the author can claim this conclusion to be true and supported by the research, much less mandated as the only possible conclusion?

After reading three cases discussed in sequence, do you know why each of those cases is mentioned? Why are those cases there? Was there a fourth case that you expected to see, but didn't? Is there something that's nagging you about a section or line of reasoning? This level of expertise is what your partner brings to his reading, without an ounce of prompting. And it's the level of expertise you are expected to have, having done the research.

A legal memorandum is not a whodunit. I do not want to be held in suspense awaiting the surprise conclusion. I really do not want the memo to raise a question in my mind early on and answer that question only later, if at all. In fact, the fewer questions a memo raises, the better; it is supposed to answer questions, not raise them.

Nor is a legal memorandum a lovely walk through the intellectual park, where we stop to smell the theoretical roses at every turn. When I read the memo, I do not want to be wondering why this case is here. I do not want to find out later (or not at all). I am busy, and impatient, and expensive. I want to know *right now.* I want the answers to leap from the page as I am reading it, without stumble or fuss. This is not just for me. It is so I will have something useful for the client, who also wants it right now.

When writing, you must anticipate the response of the reader. Identify statements that might raise questions in the mind of the reader, and answer those questions, right now.

Your memo must have a central theme, an over-arching purpose, which should be clear to the reader from the very beginning. The "very beginning" means page one, paragraph one— not page three, sub-point 14. It sounds elementary, and it is— something we're nagged about in high school, much less college—yet memo after memo wanders for page after page without providing a theme. A clear, concise, central theme. This is not make-work. It is absolutely essential. Yet even this is not enough.

Every aspect of your research, writing, and conclusions must tie directly into that central theme. "Every aspect" means every aspect. Every section, every paragraph, every sentence. If it doesn't relate directly and clearly to that central theme, your memo is not finished.

A well-thought and well-written legal memorandum holds the reader's hand throughout the entire document. No question is raised in the mind of the reader that is not immediately answered. The reader is never wondering "why is this here?" The entire memo works together in a logical progression to lead the reader inexorably to the same conclusion as the writer, who spent much more time writing it than the reader needs to spend reading it. That, after all, is the whole point of the memo.

> I asked a summer associate to research a specific point of energy regulation.
>
> The resultant memorandum was essentially a collection of quoted regulations with clever rhetorical questions interspersed. There was no explanation of what the question or even subject matter was.
>
> The summer associate had written the entire memo as if I were communing directly with her train of thought— which I was not. I had to read nearly the whole thing to even remember what project this was for, let alone what the issues were.
>
> The conclusions were logical, but the memo could only make sense to a reader who already knew exactly what she was talking about. Headache.

An essential tool to achieving this well-organized legal memorandum is a well-organized outline. Do not simply sit down and start writing from the beginning of the memo. Plan your memo. What are your conclusions? Which facts and cases relate to each conclusion? Which facts need to be presented up front, and which should be presented during discussion? In which order should the conclusions be presented? Should the conclusions be discussed in separate sections, or are they intertwined? Does the reader really need to see the heap of cases you happened across early in your research? It is in this process you will realize how cluttering much of the "research" you have done is. You must parse that mass to reach the essential law needed for that legal answer. And you must think about how that should be presented for the reader, so that she gleans the answer with an absolute minimum of effort.

These questions and more must be answered before you can start writing. Start with a rough outline, and add detail until the memo writes itself. The more detailed the outline, the easier the writing, and the better the resulting memo. Your outline might be written out in great detail or exist only in your head, but an outline you must have. This is not a pro forma exercise; you must *think* about how your memo is organized. If you are unable to develop an outline—or recreate it almost from memory—you are not ready to start writing.

A sufficient memo gives the correct answer, supported by research. A great memo is a joy to read.

Rule Number 18

Understand Your Own Memo

You have to be exact when you think, and be exact when you write. As part of this exactitude you must gain an understanding of what it is you're researching. It is pretty hard to be exact if you do not understand what you are writing.

Yet many summer associates—and actual associates—submit memos when (after the *end* of their research!) they have but the thinnest grasp of the subject material they just opined upon.

While you might sneak one by me, this is unlikely. If you do not understand—truly understand—what you are writing about, it will show. If I see even the slightest discrepancy or apparent logical flaw, I will ask you about it. Guaranteed. For that matter, I will probably ask questions about your memo even if I do not spot any flaws. If you do not truly understand the subject of your memo, chances are this will be glaringly apparent. Not good.

Therefore, understand what you are writing, and understand what you are writing about. Take the time. We know that everything is new, and that every task we give you may appear impossible. We understand that it may take you a little while to figure it out. But figure it out you must. You simply cannot try to bluff your way through.

Not only do you have to understand your memo, but you have to understand it well enough to explain it to me, and defend yourself and your memo from my questions and inquiries. You have to understand the subject matter, not just the words in your memo.

Merely understanding what is *in* the memo is not enough.

You must understand the entire memo, as well as anything I might ask you about. This means that all that secondary research and all the sources you decided were not relevant are suddenly relevant—relevant to my making sure that your conclusions are warranted. Maybe something was omitted from the memo that I expected to see. I will ask you about that. Maybe I seem to recall a case that was contrary to your conclusion. I will ask you about that. Maybe I read a bar journal article months ago that discussed a different case, or had a different take. I will ask you about that. Maybe you just reached an unexpected result. I will ask you about that.

I asked a summer associate to evaluate the client's position under a series of interrelated transaction documents. Our client wished to exit the transaction.

The memo was generally well written and well organized, and reached a good conclusion that would allow our client to terminate, but what appeared to be some minor logical glitches led me to ask questions about the research.

My interrogation quickly made it clear that there were underlying problems. The associate ultimately admitted that he did not understand the transaction or the contracts.

This had not stopped him from writing the memo.

The result was delay, embarrassment, headache, and a new memo—written by a different associate.

All those cases you cited in your memo, all those statutes, regulations? All those contract sections? I hope you are *very* familiar with them, because chances are pretty good you will need to explain those as well as what is actually in the memo.

You may be grilled far beyond what is in your memo. You need to understand the issue *thoroughly*. The memo is just the tip of your knowledge iceberg, the part you selected out for public consumption. Just because you excluded something from the memo does not mean that it is safe from inquiry. If anything, the opposite is true. Through your research *you have become the expert*. I, needing specific expertise, will call upon that special knowledge: you.

Have those cases handy, those sections tabbed. And also those other cases and sections that didn't make the final cut to be included in the memo, but were still part of the analysis. Bring it all with you when you come to my office to discuss.

I *want* to just send your memo straight to the client. That would certainly be easier for me. I don't want to do the work myself—that's why I asked you to do it. But I will pass it on only if I have confidence. Confidence in you, and confidence in your work product. Eventually you will (hopefully) earn a reputation that tells me that I can indeed trust your memo, but that will take time. Until then you have to convince me. You can convince me by delivering an excellent memo, and you can convince me again by being able to confidently answer all my questions, which you can only do if you truly understand.

Rule Number 19

Great Memo—Now Fix It

The partner is going to have comments to your memo.

This is a near-certainty. It matters not how carefully you researched and carefully you proofread. You are not me, therefore we have different thoughts/desires/expectations. Therefore, I will have comments. Maybe, some time in the future, when you can read my mind and you have a perfect grasp of the facts and the law, I will not have comments. Until then, there will be comments. This means several things to you.

First, do not take it personally.

Okay, sometimes you should take it personally. If you made a particularly obnoxious mistake, you should be embarrassed. And you should certainly take every comment seriously, and if the comment relates to an actual mistake, you should make certain not to repeat that mistake.

But quite often, the comments have nothing to do with any mistake, and merely reflect my different approach to the problem, or some fact I knew that you did not, or something that has changed, or a stylistic preference, or a million other little things that result from you not being me.

If you let the doubt gremlins get to you every time you see red ink (or its virtual equivalent), then you are going to have a very hard time as a lawyer. The law is a collaborative process. Sometimes that collaboration takes the form of friendly brainstorming, and sometimes it takes the form of me bleeding on your document and, sometimes, me getting a little agitated in my comments/concerns/critique about your work.

This is how the process works, and you need to develop the thick skin to deal with it.

Second, plan for revisions.

Revisit Rule #6—Understand The Deadline—and apply that to your planning. Now that you are expecting revisions, how does this impact your time management and planning? The stated deadline probably included some slack for revisions, but as your project shapes up, you may have a sense for just how much revision will be required. Does the nature of the research lead you to believe that there will be numerous questions and revisions? Or are you absolutely confident that no comments are possible, beyond the occasional stylistic suggestion?

Either way, you must adapt your schedule to include your revision expectations. If your memo will be extra "collaborative" (this happens sometimes, with particularly amorphous research projects), then you need to beat the actual deadline sufficiently to allow for that extra collaboration and subsequent revision.

If you are confident that your memo is flawless, then you can afford to take a little extra time, and you may be able to work closer to the real deadline.

A corollary to this, by the way, is the inverse: the later, or less early, your project is delivered, the more flawless it *must* be. If a project slips beyond the deadline, then it needs to be absolutely amazing, and more amazing yet for every day—and sometimes every hour—that goes by. You can recoup some of the ground you lost for tardiness if you deliver amazing product. You can make up for some (very minor) errors by delivering with sufficient time for the partner to review and for you to correct it. A late *and* sloppy product, on the other hand—well, just don't.

Third, you must take editing seriously.

Think of the comments you get as another whole memo. Often it may as well be a new memo, but even when the edits are less extensive, every rule in this book applies to the edits as well as to the original assignment. You must understand the purpose of the edit—the reasons and reasoning behind the partner's comments—and make it work. Partners love to scribble in margins. Notes, vague questions, random lines, squiggles, and punctuations. Ignore no scribble. Assume nothing about its meaning. Find out for sure.

> For a few months after first starting work, my standard procedure when receiving written edits was simply to hand them to my secretary to enter.
>
> I would then proofread the changes (after learning about proofreading the hard way), and merrily give the partner the revised memo.
>
> It took me several instances of second- and third-round edits to understand that editing was not a mechanical task I could outsource. Editing was my job.

If the partner has to repeat any comment for the second draft, she will not be amused. If you misinterpret a comment and do something random, she will not be amused. If you just entered the exact text she wrote in her abbreviated comment without working it into the text properly, she will not be amused. All prior rules apply with equal force to edits and revisions as they do to the first draft of the memo.

Partner comments sometimes need clarification or interpretation, particularly if they are hand-written. Remember Rule #7—Get On With It Already. Start on the edits *right away,* so that you can ask questions right away. Do not wait until late in the evening to ask the partner for an explanation (or help in reading her handwriting). Apply both Rule #3—Answer The Real Question—and Rule #4—Understand The Context—to interpreting partner comments just the same as to interpreting the original assignment.

Questions and comments provided orally must be carefully recorded and understood. It is almost more important to be clear on the edits than on the original assignment, because there is more potential for mischief on the edits. You might well be sick and tired of this stupid memo by now (and the partner might well be fidgeting over the deadline), and the temptation to "just finish it" can be overwhelming. Before you know it you are liberally interpreting comments just to be done with it, rather than making sure that you understand the thrust (or importance) of the comment. Or, just as bad, you are blindly entering the marked changes without understanding the impact on the whole document or reasoning behind that change. You must consider the document as a whole, and if a change leads to other changes, then you must also make those other changes.

If the question is different after revisions than it was before, which it often will be, then you have a new question—which means you have a new memo, which means all rules must be applied afresh. Editing is not make-work. It is not pro forma. Make sure that your revised memo answers the revised question, exactly.

Editing is not something you do to modify your finished product. This is not the partner putting his stamp of approval on your work. You cannot abdicate responsibility for your memo just because the partner required you to make changes. Your memo is not finished when you hand it to me, and neither is your responsibility. Your memo is finished when *I* say it is, not before, and you should take the last change as seriously as the very first word.

Rule Number 20

You Are The Expert

There you are, a fresh law school graduate. Or perhaps still a student in law school. You just survived final exams and perhaps the bar exam. You are at the law office, surrounded by dozens or hundreds of lawyers with more experience than you—not difficult, since you have zero experience. Some of these lawyers were, as the saying goes, practicing law since before you were born, and they all have a vastly greater grasp of law practice and the practicalities of law and business than you can comprehend from your new, lowly station.

And they are asking you for *your* advice.

Not only are they asking you for advice, but they plan on following your advice. They will do this, not because they want you to feel good about yourself, or as a training exercise. They will do this because, on this particular point, on this issue, at this time, you are the expert.

You are the expert.

You did the research. You reviewed the facts and the law. At this moment, if you have done your job right, you are the *preeminent expert in your entire firm on this particular matter*. You. Nobody else is in your position of knowledge and understanding. Thus, despite your general status as neophyte underling, all eyes are on you to provide the answer. As shocking as it may be, the partners are relying on *you* to advise Fortune 500 companies regarding multi-million-dollar (and bigger) decisions.

What this means, primarily, is that no one else will provide the answer. There is no safety net. *You* are the safety net. Act accordingly.

It also means something else. Let us say you finished the memo. You finally, *finally,* finished the memo. Understood, researched, written, delivered. The end.

No.

A finished memo is rarely the end. An attorney's job rarely has an "end." There are always follow-ups. Renegotiations. Amendments. Appeals. Revisiting old research for a slightly different project, or for the same client's next project. Revisiting old research for a slightly different project for a new client. If nothing else, a question will come up in an unrelated case that will have issues similar to those you researched.

Handing over the final memo to the partner is the beginning, not the end.

The case or transaction does not end because you finished your memo. The memo goes into the casefile, and every time there is a new motion on a related point, your memo will get pulled out and reviewed. If there are any questions on the issue, you will get the call. You are still the expert.

> Due to my work with other clients, I worked on a maritime transaction as a mid-level associate (with the assistance of experienced maritime lawyers), despite having no prior exposure to maritime issues. The transaction involved the writing of several memoranda on issues of maritime law.
>
> Based on this single transaction and handful of memos, maritime matters were referred to me for years, regardless of the presence of actual shipping law experts in our firm.

I am still defending or discussing memos I wrote more than a decade ago, or at least the subject matters of those memos. Transactions may close, but the files do not go away, and somebody will remember (or find out) that I worked on "a deal kind of like this one" a few years back. That makes me the expert, and I will get the call.

This is not a bad thing. It is a good thing. A very good thing. A legal memo is not just a "project." When you write a legal memo, you are building your practice and your expertise. This is, moreover, very much a two-way street. I regularly call upon colleagues who have written memos that might help a current client of mine; every little bit helps, and an old memo is a solid start to any new issue.

This is not just a task. This is your career. Ultimately, the main beneficiary of your memo is not the partner or the client, but you.

Rule Number 21

Have Fun!

That's right. Have fun.

You just read twenty rules full of stern lecture, but perhaps the most welcome advice I can give is to have fun.

In many ways, the legal memorandum encapsulates all that is lawyerdom: the quest for knowledge, the careful analysis of information, the formation of arguments, the endless give-and-take with colleagues and adversaries alike, the sage advice to the client. While you might find yourself doing fewer and fewer memos as you proceed along your career path, the underlying foundations of the legal memo will be with you for as long as you practice law. Instead of preparing them you will be directing them, and instead of learning bits and pieces you will be absorbing the accumulated knowledge in each. This *is* fun.

As a result, you should find enjoyment in these quests, for otherwise you will have an unhappy career, and very possibly an even more unhappy life.

I have faith—you made it far enough into the law that you are in a position to need this book, which most likely means that you are exactly the kind of person who can indeed enjoy the challenges and rewards that lawyers face daily.

If, that is, you let yourself enjoy them.

All too often attorneys, both junior and senior, get so wrapped up in the seriousness of the task at hand that they do not allow themselves to appreciate the beauty of the moment.

It's okay to have fun. In fact, it will make you a better lawyer.

Good luck.

ABOUT THE AUTHOR

Morten Lund is a partner with the law firm of Foley & Lardner LLP, where he practices in renewable energy development and finance.

He attended Augustana College (the one in Rock Island) and Yale Law School. He lives in a quiet suburb with his family, and has been thoroughly taken in by the poker craze.

He is a voracious reader of epic fantasy fiction, and has several works of his own in process, some of which may even be finished some day.

INDEX

OTHER BOOKS

NON-LAW ADVENTURES

GRAINS OF GOLDEN SAND: ADVENTURES IN WAR-TORN AFRICA,
by Delfi Messinger
Hardcover 978-1-888960-35-8,
391 pages, US$21.95
Softcover 1-888960-33-4,
391 pages, US$15.95

Grab a ticket for the adventure of a
lifetime: meet a woman who protects
rare apes by painting, in blood, SIDA
("AIDS" in French) on a Kinshasa
wall to keep rampaging looters at bay.

Her mission was to save a small group of endangered great apes—the
bonobo (or "sexy" ape)—from the grip of civil war in the heart of Zaire.
She made this her mission, and after eight harrowing years the reader
will be breathless with amazement in her struggles to get the endangered
animals to safety.

TRAINING WHEELS FOR STUDENT LEADERS: A JUNIOR COUNSELING
PROGRAM IN ACTION, by Autumn Messinger
ISBN 978-1-888960-13-6, US$21.95

A reference for the engaged parent,
founded on the premise that, if given the
opportunity, mentoring, and guidance,
even young children can work together
to solve (and resolve) their own
problems. They can work towards their
own, common, cooperative goals. They
can build genuine self-esteem.

In two very different schools hundreds of students achieved far more
than they, their parents, their teachers, or the administrators ever
thought was possible. This will improve performance and (real) self-
esteem, it will make true counseling possible for overworked school staff,
and it will connect students to their community. Parents should demand
this, while administrators should support a program that produces truly
astonishing self-reliance and self-motivation among students.

LATER-IN-LIFE LAWYERS: TIPS FOR THE NON-TRADITIONAL LAW STUDENT,
by Charles Cooper
ISBN 978-1-888960-06-8, 288 pages,
US$18.95

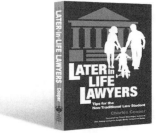

Law school is a scary place for any new
student. For an older ("non-traditional")
student, it can be intimidating as well
as ill-designed for the needs of a student
with children, mortgages, and the
like. Includes advice on families and
children; the LSAT, GPAs, application
process, and law school rankings for
non-traditional students; paying for law school; surviving first year;
non-academic hurdles; and the occasional skeleton in the non-
traditional closet. This book is a must-read for the law student who is
not going directly from college to law school...and offers an important
perspective for even traditional students going through 19 straight
years of education.

THE SLACKER'S GUIDE TO LAW SCHOOL: SUCCESS WITHOUT STRESS,
by Juan Doria
ISBN 978-1-888960-52-5, 162 pages,
US$16.95

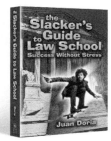

It is easy to fall into a trap of assuming
that one either strives and succeeds or
slacks and fails. Enjoying three years
of law school is not the opposite of
learning the law. There's also a tendency
to follow a herd mentality: the
assumption that there's just one right
way to do something, or just one way to
study the law. Too often, this involves too much make-work and too
much stress. This book will show you how to do law school right:
success without stress. (Or at least with *less* stress.)

FOR THE LAW STUDENT

LAW SCHOOL: GETTING IN, GETTING GOOD, GETTING THE GOLD,
by Thane Messinger
ISBN: 978-1-888960-80-8, 367 pages,
US$16.95

The key in successful law study is a minimum
of wasted effort and a maximum of results. Still
outlining cases? A waste of time. Failing to use
hypotheticals? A dangerous omission.
Preparing a huge outline? A dangerous waste
of time. Don't waste your time, and don't neglect what's truly
important. Learn law school techniques that work. Once you're in, Get
Good, and Get the Gold!

THE INSIDER'S GUIDE TO GETTING A BIG FIRM JOB: WHAT EVERY LAW
STUDENT SHOULD KNOW ABOUT INTERVIEWING,
by Erika M Finn and Jessica T. Olmon
ISBN-13 978-1-888960-14-3, 130 pages,
US$16.95

The competition for top jobs is intense, and the
special needs of law firm recruiters are
unknown to most law students. Most books
aimed at law students speak to how to get into
law school, and how to succeed in law school, but none address how to
get a lucrative job. This book is an insider's look at the secrets of land-
ing a dream law firm job.

PLANET LAW SCHOOL II: WHAT YOU NEED TO KNOW (BEFORE YOU GO)—
BUT DIDN'T KNOW TO ASK...AND NO ONE ELSE WILL TELL YOU,
by Atticus Falcon
ISBN 978-1-888960-50-7, 858 pages, US$24.95

An encyclopedic reference. Examines hundreds
of sources, and offers in-depth advice on law
courses, materials, methods, study guides, professors, attitude, examsmanship, law review,
internships, research assistantships, clubs, clin-
ics, law jobs, dual degrees, advanced law
degrees, MBE, MPRE, bar review options, and the bar exam. Sets out
all that a law student must master to excel in law school.

Jagged Rocks of Wisdom: Professional Advice for the new Attorney,
by Morten Lund
ISBN: 978-1-888960-07-5, US$18.95

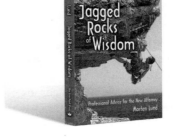

Written by a real-world mentor at a
national law firm, this no-nonsense
guide is a must-have guide for the new
associate. Its "21 Rules of Law Office
Life" will help make the difference to
your success in the law: surviving your
first years as an attorney, and making
partner. Beware. Avoid the dangers.
Read, read, and read again these 21 Rules of Law Office Life.

The Young Lawyer's Jungle Book: A Survival Guide,
by Thane Messinger
ISBN 978-1-888960-19-1,
231 pages, US$18.95

A career guide for summer associates,
judicial clerks, and all new attorneys.
Now in its 12th year and second edition,
hundreds of sections with advice on law
office life, advice on law office life,
including working with senior attorneys,
legal research and writing, memos,
contract drafting, mistakes, grammar, email, managing workload,
timesheets, annual reviews, teamwork, department, attitude, perspective,
working with clients (and dissatisfied clients), working with office staff,
using office tools, and yes, much more.

Recommended in the ABA's *Law Practice Management* and *The
Compleat Lawyer,* as well as in numerous state bar journals.